THE LATINO VOTE

The Future of American Politics

Jorge S. Olson

Table of Contents

Introduction

Driving to Los Angeles from San Diego, California I stopped at a fast food restaurant to get coffee. It can be a two-and-a-half-hour drive to a four-hour drive depending on traffic on the 4 or 405 freeway. The attendant wore a name tag with Maria written in big letters.
"What would you like?" she said flashing a happy smile.
"Buenos Dias (good morning)," I said in Spanish.
"Buenos Dias senor (good morning sir)," she answered.

Then she proceeded to take my order. I counted five people that I could see from the counter including what I could see of the kitchen. All speaking in Spanish or a mix of Spanish and English. The ladies at the counter spoke perfect English without a Mexican accent except for one of them. I noticed her accent, but other than that her speech was perfect.

If you live in Los Angeles, in San Diego, Chicago, anywhere in Texas or Florida, you probably have an ear for Spanish and maybe even some friends or family, colleagues or clients who speak it. In some of these States we have Latinos, especially Mexican Americans, as the majority of the population in only one more generation. In California, Latinos are already the Ethnic majority since 2014 with Caucasians a close second. But the gap is growing. What does this mean for politics? The answer is not as simple as you might think. At first glance you would probably say that all these votes will go to the Democratic Party. However, most Latinos are conservative by nature. They vote democrat because it's the party for minorities. "How can I vote Republican if their candidate threatens to deport my parents?" one Latina voter asked me.

The US House of Representatives has 53 seats from California from the overall 435 available and only 14 are Republicans. To put this into perspective, Vermont and Delaware have one representative each. As more Latino voters influence the California law makers, the power of the Latino vote will be heard across the nation, not just in the Latinos most populous states.

Even heavily favorite Republican states such as Texas, with two Republicans as Senators, one of them, Ted Cruz, running for president in 2016, have a growing Latino shadow in politics. In the House of Representatives 25 seats are Republican and 10 are Democrats. Of those democratic seats only two are non-minority. This also points to a trend where according to the US Census Bureau 38.6% of the state population is Latino to 43.5% white. What will happen to Texas when Latinos become the population majority and then the voting majority? That will depend entirely on the approach of both parties to Latinos and other minorities. Stating they are pro-Latino or pro-Hispanic is not enough. Especially in southern states that feel every anti-Latino, anti-Mexican, and anti-immigration statements as a jab, a right hook, and an uppercut.

The immigration divide between parties was not always as black and white, as Democrat and Republican as it seems today. Presidents Ronald Reagan, George H. W. Bush and George W. Bush were very friendly towards immigrants from the south. President Reagan did his best to negotiate with his party and provide amnesty to three million undocumented immigrants. Opinions vary on his Immigration Reform and Control Act of 1986 (IRCA). Where along with amnesty came stronger border enforcement to deter more immigration. However, research paints a different picture of Reagan, one of an open border where people and trade can flow. This goes in line with his invisible hand capitalistic views.

"Reagan himself was a dreamer, capable of imagining a world without trade barriers. In announcing his presidential candidacy in Nov. 1979, he had proposed a "North American accord" in which commerce & people would move freely across the borders of Canada & Mexico".
From the book: President Reagan: The Role of a Lifetime. Page 461 by Lou Cannon. Printed by Simon and Schuster Feb 1 1992.

I was at an investor's conference in New Orleans speaking with passersby when a man approached our booth.

"Tell me about your fund," he said.

"We're creating a venture capital fund for investing in Mexico," I started explaining.

"Investing in Mexico?" He asked cringing. "Why would you want to invest in Mexico if all the Mexicans are coming here illegally?" he said, shaking his head in obvious disapproval. His tone was angry and his face contoured into a dried prune.

"What should I say?" I thought. "Should I make a witty remark? Explain the GDP of Mexico, the immigration statistics, the culture? How about the Social Security surplus of $100 million left by those illegals? No, this would just escalate things," I thought. I smiled at him. "Have a good conference," I said. "If ignorance is bliss, this man is a saint," I thought while walking away.

A month later I found myself at a private club in New York. Not a dance club mind you, but the type of club investment bankers and hedge fund managers go to rub shoulders in high end custom suits and twenty thousand dollar wristwatches. I was a guest of a potential client. There he introduced me to business owners and some of the investment community elite.

"Jorge," one of them said. "What kind of name is that?"
"It's a Spanish name," I answered. "In my case it was given to me via Mexico from my mother," I explained.

"Oh, you're Mexican?" he asked.

"I was born and raised in Mexico," I said. "My father is American."

"My maid is Mexican," he told me proudly.

"That's nice," I said grinning, smile frozen in place. I'm no stranger to this type of conversation.

"Her name is Maria," he told me proudly. "But she's not here illegally," he made clear.

Again, I just smiled not knowing if I should tell him an illegal in New York doesn't scare me. Or if I should inquire about his maid. Maybe he thinks we have something in common because he employs a maid. Would it be a difference if he tells me, "My doctor is Mexican. Or my attorney is Mexican. Or my Boss, the owner of the firm, is Mexican." Would he even know his Attorney is Latino if he saw a tall blond Jewish man born in Mexico City? Probably not until he listened to his Spanish. Not knowing the answer to these questions is part of the problem. It's part of not understanding the culture and now knowing how to relate to it.

I'm sure the man I spoke with didn't mean anything by his comment. As I'm sure the man in New Orleans didn't either. Just like many political candidates they don't understand the language, the culture or even how to engage in small talk conversation. What happens here? Where is the disconnect? Why can movies, products, and services target Latinos while politicians, especially on the right, miss the mark?

The answer is easy to find but very difficult to apply

Latinos represent many countries from Mexico to Argentina and every country in between. It's a land mass larger than the US with a population of double the size. Each country sharing a language (except for Brazil and small islands) but with different customs, music, food and lifestyles. In the USA, many white Americans only notice their contact with Latinos when they can tell them apart by racial or socioeconomic divides. Such as a brown construction worker, the maid working in a hotel, or the field worker picking vegetables. Here the brain starts associating blue collar jobs with a particular color, language skills, and socioeconomic background. The brain then prejudges using what it knows when they meet someone wearing a Latino name, such as mine, Jorge. If all previous associations with the name and its implications points to blue collar, that sticks.

On the contrary, if your university classmates are Latinos, smart, and get higher grades than you, they get promotions faster at the workplace and make more money, the same individual will associate Latino with smart, white collar, hard working. However, one strong identifier is missing. If this same white collar executive is of fair skin and tall of stature our white friend might not see them as Latino. I've had such conversations where people ask me "How come you're taller than me," or tell me "You're not a real Latino," or "Your English is very good". For which I usually respond, "Yours is good as well". What happens here? Simple, I don't fit into their criteria of what a Latino or a Mexican American should look like.

It's difficult to separate the Latino vote from immigration issues. First because many Latinos or their ancestors immigrated to the USA. Note I say many, but not all, as annexation of southwestern states into the union appropriated many Mexicans that instantly became Mexican-Americans. Secondly because the issue is present in many national political campaigns. Bunching up immigrants with Latinos and building walls to keep them out all in the same sentence.

Having an honest conversation about Latinos, immigration and the future of US politics will strike an emotional reaction in many people. However, a conversation is what the country and politicians need in order to understand and adapt to the largest growing segment of the population, economy and political influence.

In this book we'll explore the history of Latino immigration, both legal and not, as well as the definition of both legal and illegal immigration. We'll peek into the mind of the average Latino to see what they think about politics and ask them about their political inclination, how they relate to the parties, do they feel included or excluded from the political process, and their message to politicians. We'll even dive into the tags as well as the myths of the Latino population. Discovering why we're called Latinos even if we don't speak Latin!

Understanding the Latino population and its diversity will create better legislation, political campaigns, and even dialog from both parties with each other and with the growing Latino population.

PART I

KNOW YOUR MARKET

Part I will focus on understanding the voter, the target market, the person we want to influence and sell on our policy, on campaign contributions, and to get their vote.

Businesses use Target Marketing to segment and identify the group of people or even the person you want as your customer. More seasoned marketers call this your Avatar. An Avatar is your ideal client and you have to know everything about them. Not just their income level, age, and political preference; I mean everything. You have to know what they think, how they feel, what's important to them, where they come from and where they are going. This is what we'll learn about the Latino Voter.

"To Get the Vote, You Need to Understand the Voter!"

Voting Power: The Changing Color of America

The growth of Latinos impacts national politics exponentially. Yes, the Latino vote is present in state and local elections, however the impact is much greater in positions that influence national policy such as presidential and congressional elections.

This chapter will show how the growing population of Latinos will affect local, state, and national elections. Because Latinos grow more in large metropolitan areas in states with many electoral votes and congressman the influence will grow faster than the population.

Let's dig into this concept to see how the Latinos influence is exponential. On the surface Latinos are a growing majority but still a minority nationwide. In reality they are a majority in large States, in those that carry many electoral votes and have an overwhelming majority of congress representatives. What does this mean? It means that by voting in key States, Latinos can change national policy.

In July 8, 2015 the newspaper LA Times declared "It's official: Latinos now outnumber whites in California". This is not just true in California. In an article published on July 6th 2015 by US News they wrote:

"Minorities will outnumber whites in the USA in one generation according to the Census Bauru. According to the U.S. Census Bureau, in 2014 there were more than 20 million children under 5 years old living in the U.S., and 50.2 percent of them were minorities.

Parents who identified their child as white with Hispanic origin were the largest minority, making up 22 percent of the 19.9 million children under age 5, followed by African American children, who make up 15 percent."
US News

Sometime in 2013, there was a hint that soon Latinos would outnumber whites to form the largest ethnic group within California, but demographers could not confirm that until new population figures were announced by the Census Bureau. However, demographers were not wrong and the puzzle to determining whether Latinos have outnumbered whites in California was solved when finally, the Census Bureau released the new population figures in the summer of 2014.

In the new tally, it was found that as of July 1, 2014, approximately 14.99 million Latinos reside in California thereby edging out the white's population in the state, which at that time stood at 14.92 million. While this may not have come as a surprise because demographers had previously shed some light on the emerging changes in demography between the Latinos and white's population in

California sometime in 2013, however, this shows that California and some other states are witnessing an important change in demographics that could have a big influence on the political scene in the nation.

In fact, demographers cited that the change could have occurred in 2013 but owing to a slow population growth, the projections about the shift in population was pushed back. Regardless of the timing or whether the demographers were right or wrong on such projections, the moment seems to have finally come.

As director of the Tomás Rivera Policy Institute at USC Roberto Suro said, "This is sort of the official statistical recognition of something that has been underway for almost an entire generation."[1]

According to officials, California has now become the first larger state and in overall, the third state without a white plurality after New Mexico and Hawaii. The Latino population in America as of 2015 is estimated to be about 55.4 million, and Los Angeles County and California are cited to have the largest population of Latinos than any other county or state in the country, as new figures reveal. This demographic shift has been waited for, for a long period of time.

According to state figures, in 1970, the Latino population that was tallied reached about 2.4 million representing 12 percent of the California population. In that time, the white's population was estimated to be 15.5 million and made up more than 75 percent or three-quarters of the residents of the state. By 1990, a seemingly unexpected trend in population changes was witnessed. The Latino population increased to reach 7.7 million in 1990 taking a share of a quarter or 25 percent of California's population.[2]

However, at present, the Latino population is quite young having a median age of roughly 29 while the white's population in California seems to be aging and is estimated to have a median age of 45. This has an implication on growth of the population of Latinos considering that, this is an age that is within the bracket of a productive population in terms of bearing children.

Also, state demographers are projecting that Latinos will grow exponentially to account for close to 49 percent of California's population by 2060. Suro further says that the population is actually going to accelerate and what we may be witnessing is just the beginning of a new chapter that is going to play out in the next coming generation.

The effects of the growing population of Latinos will not only be experienced in the political scenes, but also in social economic spheres of life in California. For example, a chief demographer serving in the state finance department John Malson has said that a young Latino workforce will help the economy by taking up the positions of retiring baby boomers.[3]

While some people have argued that the growth of the Latino population in the United States has been fueled by immigrants, on the other hand, according to a professor who is also the dean of education for Graduate School of Education and Information Studies at University of California, Los Angeles (UCLA) Marcelo Suárez-Orozco, he pointed out that the influx and increased growth of Latinos in the U.S. is not particularly being fueled by only immigration but also by the so called second and third generation Latino immigrants who are now settling down and starting their families.[4]

One key factor when it comes to understanding the wide views and experiences from Latinos in the USA is how long these people and their families have lived in the country. Generally speaking, the Hispanics in the U.S. are very diverse and they cover a range of populations from those immigrants who recently arrived in the country to the Latinos whose ancestors have resided in the United States for many generations.

Latinos are thus divided into three generations or groups of populations. There is the first generation of Latinos who are categorized as those who were born outside the U.S. and a second generation consisting of the Latinos who were born in the U.S. to immigrant parents. A third generation is that which is made up of Latinos who are said to have been born in U.S. to parents born in the country.

Understanding how these generations perceive their identity and the attitudes they possess regarding social and political values can form a good basis for understanding the Latino voters. California is demonstrating a phase of nationwide increase in Latino population. Since 2000, the Latino population in the U.S. has increased by 57 percent.[5] In 2000, Latinos were estimated to be 35.3 million and today they are anticipated to be 55.4 percent.[6]

According to Pew Research Center, the Latino population accounts for the majority of the country's growth by recording a 56 percent growth from the year 2000 to 2010.[7] Suárez-Orozco further noted that, what we are seeing in Los Angeles is what is going to happen to the rest of California and the country at large. Suárez-Orozco said that "Where L.A. goes is where the rest of the state goes and where the rest of the country goes," further adding "We announce, demographically speaking, the future for the rest of the country."[8]

While the number of Hispanic votes in 2016 is expected to reach a record high, there are however skepticisms as to whether that could bring any impact on the national elections. More than 27 million Hispanics are eligible to vote, a number that nearly outweighs the population of African-Americans in the U.S. as per a report released by

Pew Research Center on 19 January 2016.[9] The Hispanic populations appears to skew so young in such a way that it is unlikely to have a big impact when it comes to the elections.

It is estimated that about 44 percent of the Hispanic population is categorized as the millennials— those who were born after 1980.[10] This could mean that this group is less likely to participate in elections or they don't register to cast their vote when compared to the older Hispanics who have a different perception, attitude, and opinions when it comes to political issues.

The projected number of eligible Hispanic voters being tallied as 27.3 million for the 2016 elections is so far the greatest of any other ethnic or racial group of voters. The Hispanic millennials among the 27.3 million projected Hispanic eligible voters will account for close to half (to be precise 44 percent) of that eligible voter number according to the January 2016 report by Pew Research Center that analyzed the US Census Bureau data.[11]

The youth in the so called U.S.-born Hispanic population has a large footprint of millennial Latinos who are eligible voters. Such a young population is going to be a key factor when it comes to voter influence among the Latinos. Among the country's 35 million Latinos born in the US, their median age is only 19.[12] This means that this population is going to start voting and may become a big driver for the Latino eligible voter's growth over the coming two decades. About 3.2 million young Latinos who are U.S. citizens will have progressed to attain adulthood thereby becoming eligible to cast their vote between 2012 and 2016, according to projections by the Pew Research Center.[13] This may be seen as the largest pool of the growth of Hispanic electorate, however, it is not the only source of increased eligible Hispanics voter population.

Another group is the adult Hispanic immigrants regarded as legal immigrants and who have decided to become citizens of U.S. by naturalization. In the years between 2012 and 2016, it had been projected that about 1.2 million adult Hispanic immigrants will have become citizens of the U.S. by naturalization.[14] There has also been another group which is likely to add on to the eligible Hispanics voter group— this is the outmigration population that comes from Puerto Rico. From 2012, an estimated 130,000 Puerto Ricans are said to have left the island and Florida has been receiving a larger number of these adult migrants.[15] These migrants are all U.S. citizens and therefore, they are eligible to cast their vote in U.S. elections.

The Latino voter turnout may be lower than what is expected considering that a large number of eligible voters are millennials, nonetheless, the increasing number of immigrant Latinos who are U.S. citizens may advance the voter turnout rates for Latinos. However, it is not clear whether the Hispanic community is going to be organized and energized to turn out for voting owing to the shift of the political stand in regard to immigration.

While remarks by one of the key Republican front runners in the presidential campaign of 2016, Donald Trump may have infuriated most people in the Hispanic community by making sediments that did not go well with the community, that may or may not influence the Latino's willingness and ability to vote. The remarks were denounced by other Republicans, however, most of the Republicans continued to call for more border security including the completion of the wall running along the southwest border. The Republicans called for stepping up of deportations of close to 11 million undocumented immigrants believed to be residing in the United States.[16] The recent political game touching on the Hispanic community may have an impact on the overall voting rate. Besides the increasing population of eligible voter Hispanics in the nation, the community is also becoming educated.

The number of Hispanics holding a bachelor's degree or higher academic achievements, and who are eligible to cast votes, has climbed from about 11 percent to close to 18 percent from 2000 to 2016 respectively. High school dropouts among the Hispanics eligible to vote in the U.S. has also reduced from 32 percent to about 20 percent within the same period.[17]

There have also been notable increases in eligible voters of Hispanic origin among various presidential swing states, and these could help in deciding the election voting results. In Florida for example, Hispanics are going to take up 18.1 percent of the eligible voters while in Nevada, they will take up 17.2 percent of the eligible voters and in Colorado, they take 14.5 percent share of the eligible voters.[18]

Florida is one state that has been perceived as a battleground in presidential elections considering that Hispanic voters are now playing a big role in determining who is who in the presidential vote. In 2016, Hispanic voters in Florida made up a larger share of the registered voters in the state when compared to last year, 2015. However, the profile of Latino votes has been taking a different twist over the last decade.

Florida has a big block of Cuban voters and in the past, Latino vote had presumably been taken up by the Republicans. In 2004, for example President George W. Bush clinched the win for both the Hispanic vote as well as the state vote. However, a tipping point occurred in 2008 when a wave of change was witnessed among the registered voters.

In that year, more Latinos registered as Democrats when compared to those registered as Republicans. This made a historic shift in the party preferences of the Hispanics.

Before 2008, Hispanics mainly preferred to register as Republicans but this year saw a turn of events.

Surprisingly, the gap of Hispanics registering as Democrats and those registering as Republicans since 2008 has only continued to widen. This trend caused a growing influence of the Democrats in not only the state vote but also the Hispanic vote in 2008 and 2012. These are the periods when presidential elections went in favor of Barack Obama— who garnered the highest number of Hispanic and state votes.

There has also been another group of Latinos who do not affiliate themselves with any party. The number of Hispanic registered voters in the state of Florida who are not affiliated to any party has also been rapidly growing. By 2012, the number has actually surpassed the Hispanics registered with the Republican Party. Florida is the third largest Hispanic populated state after California and Texas and in 2014, it had a Hispanic population of about 4.8 million.

About 24 percent of Florida population is Hispanics as of 2014 compared to 17 percent in 2000. As of February 2016, close to 1.8 million Hispanics are granted the right to vote in Florida by becoming registered voters, according to information from the Division of Elections in the state. Among the Florida population, the number of registered democrats outweighed Republicans as of 2016. One of the contributing factors to this trend is the Hispanics who accounted for about 88 percent of the increase recorded in registered Democrats from 2006 to 2016.[19]

In the same period, the figures of registered Hispanic voters in Florida showed an increase by about 61 percent, and those identifying themselves as Democrats increased by about 83 percent. Those with no party affiliation also increased by about 95 percent. While the number of Hispanic registered voters in the state of Florida registered as Republicans has also been increasing, the pace has been much slow with only an increase of about 16 percent.[20]

In the Hispanic population that obtained voter registration in 2016, about 678,000 choose to associate with Democrats while about 610,000 indicated that they had no party affiliation. About 479,000 Hispanic registered voters in Florida in 2016 associated themselves with Republicans.[21] While these figures may give some suggestions on the direction the elections in the state is likely to take, it is imperative to note that among all registered voters, not everyone may be able to cast a ballot. Also, the voter turnout could somewhat impact on the results in this swing state.

In the county of Miami-Dade in southeastern Florida, which is considered home to over 46 percent of the state's Cuban American population, it appeared that Republicans outweighed Democrats in regard to Hispanic registered voters. There were about 260,000 Republicans while the Democrats were 213,000 as of 2016.[22] These figures however showed a decreased number of Hispanic registered voters associating themselves with the parties where there was a reduction of close to 5000 people from the 2014 figures. Nonetheless, statewide trends seem to be holding true despite this Cuban stronghold where figures for Hispanic registered voters from 2006 to 2016 showed that there was an increase of the Democrats by 62 percent while on the other hand, the number of the Republicans was flat.

The question as to how effective the increasing population is going to impact on the 2016 voting results lies on how the ethnic community is going to be mobilized. *Have presidential candidates and other state representatives taken the bull by the horns to energize and influence the Latinos to cast their votes?*

While in California, the Latinos recently surpassed whites to form the largest ethnic group, that number may not impact the vote results if Hispanics do not vote. Let's look back and see how things have happened in the past. In 2014, for example, Latinos only represented about 15 percent of the population eligible to vote in California yet only 17 percent of the entire population of Latinos granted the right to vote (meaning the Hispanic eligible voters) actually voted.

For the first time, a majority of registered voters in California will be primarily minority voters in 2016. In essence, how Latinos are going to be mobilized and in particular the millennials who form a larger part of the growing Latino voters may help determine the voting results in a number of states in the 2016 election and even the years to come. The interesting part is that, if Latinos maintain the trend in turnout rate for voting that was experienced in California during the 2012 elections, where only about 39.4 percent of eligible registered voters casted their vote, there may be no significant changes in the outcome of the results.

Latino electorate has for decades leaned towards the side of the Democratic Party in regard to presidential elections and it is one of the demographically dynamic groups in California. The population of Latinos is not only growing fast but also increasingly becoming college-educated. It's ability to influence the nation's battleground states in the 2016 elections has also increased considering that the Hispanic population has become a bit dispersed countrywide and grown in numbers in particular key states.

Unless the political influence of the Latinos is properly understood and politicians take the right approach to reach out to this group and market themselves, the Latino voters may just go unnoticed. They may not vote as expected and this could again mean that the influence on presidential and state representative votes may not be felt.

Despite the projected increased number of the Latino electorate in 2016, which makes the ethnic population to be poised to bring a large impact on presidential elections, for some reason, those Latino voters might again (as has happened in the past) be underrepresented among voters when compared to their share in the eligible voters in the nation or their share in the entire national population. The voter turnout for Hispanic registered voters has not been impressive in the past and this is a trend likely to be seen in 2016 elections.

If Hispanics can cast their vote in the key battleground states of the nation, this could have a big impact on not only the Congress representatives, but more importantly on the national elections meaning that they could form a big block that is capable of changing and influencing the national policy.

Latino population is growing but it's not just growing; the importance of growth is not just that there will be more voters. The way U.S. politics are arranged, the most influence is in Congress and in presidential election. Depending on the state you live in, you can get the most influence.

If Latinos are spread over the United States, they will have the same influence in percentage as everyone else, however, if you concentrate on the same population in large states that have a lot of electorates and a lot of representatives then the influence is likely to be much greater.

For example, if you take the largest states where Latinos are growing and you examine members of Congress in those states, you can see how Latinos can influence policy making and law making in the U.S. while still being a minority in the country. States growing in Latino population are Texas, New Mexico, Arizona, California, Nevada, Oregon, Washington, Colorado, Nebraska, Florida, Illinois, New York, and New Jersey. You will notice some of these have a lot of representation in Congress such as California with 53 members representing 12 percent of the entire Congress, followed by Texas with 36 members that is 8 percent, Florida 6 percent, and New York 6 percent.

If you add the states I mentioned, there is a big percentage majority in Congress. This means that as more Latinos are active in politics, and we are not taking about Latinos in two, three or five years to come, but the existing Latinos right now; they will have a big impact on the Congress and presidential election. If they are voting, because that is the problem— a lot of them are not voting; there will be a big influence. If they are politically aware and register to vote and start voting, things could change greatly in elections. These are just Latinos who can vote in those states— where they are growing the most. If you only take those states, they can influence policy and control the Congress.

How is this possible if they're still a growing minority?

Congress is by population and by coincident, Latinos are growing more in the United States, and the same states have the most electoral votes. So the same thing will happen in presidency. We will have a massive, massive influence in the next election and future elections.

Latino Voter: Get The Facts

The United States is going through a big historic demographic change, with minorities estimated to make up a preponderance of the population by 2044. The most significant of theses shifts is the sharp increase in the number of Latino voters and their share of the electorate. Close to 71 percent of Latino voters who supported President Barack Obama in the 2012 presidential elections helped create a bulwark for President Obama in key states. The climbing number of Latino voters in primary states could have even more influence on the presidential election of 2016, especially if the attendance rates of voters are high.[23]

On September 17, 1787,[24] the nation's founders signed the Constitution of the United States. On this date every year, the Americans celebrate Constitution Day, which is also referred to as Citizenship Day. President Barack Obama established the White House Task Force on new Americans to improve the civic, economic, and linguistic integration of immigrants and refugees by launching *the Citizenship Public Education and Awareness Campaign.* This campaign promotes the importance of U.S. citizenship and provides free citizenship preparation resources for those eligible to become citizens. In honor of these occasions, there are important facts about Latinos and their voting power.

1. Latino electorate in U.S. is steadily increasing

About 16 percent of the adult population in the U.S. will be Latinos aged 18 and above as of 2016. By 2016, there will be nearly 39.8 million Latinos over 18 years in U.S. as per the U.S. Census Bureau predictions. It is also estimated that about 800,000 Latinos attain the age of 18 each year — translating to one Latino turning 18 every 30 seconds.[25] There are about 33 percent Latino children who are U.S. – born citizens and these will be entitled to take part in voting when they grow to be 18.

As of 2014, it was estimated that one in four children (about 17.6 million in total) were Latinos. What this means is that minorities are nearly making up the majority of the population of under 18 in the country. The percentage of Latinos under age of 18 in relation to the U.S. population under age 18 is expected to rise from 24 percent recorded in 2014 to about 33 percent or more by 2060.[26]

2. The number of Latinos in U.S. is growing

By 2016, there will be an estimated 58.1 million Latinos in the United States, which is an increase from the most recent population estimates of 55.4 million in 2014, making up 17.4% of the population. Between 2014 and 2060, the Latino population is expected to increase by 115% to some 119 million, which will cover about 29% of the U.S. population.[27]

3. The Latino share of eligible voters is growing

Latinos are likely to make up 13% of eligible voters in 2016, which is a 2 percent increase from 2012. For example, in Florida, the share of eligible Latino voters will upsurge from 17 percent in 2012 to 20.2 percent in 2016. In Nevada, the eligible Latino voters increased from 15.9 percent to 18.8 percent. This goes to show that the eligible Latino voters could extend to 28.5 million nationwide in 2016.[28]

4. Latinos are not really emphasized regarding registered voter rolls

There were 13.7 million Latinos who were registered to vote in 2012. However, despite the fact that 23.3 million Latinos were eligible to vote that year, 41 percent were eligible to vote but did not register. And this does not include those that could naturalize but have not. About 8.8 million permanent residents by law were authorized to become citizens as of 2013 but had not acclimatized.[29]

5. Latinos are increasingly showing up in greater numbers at the polls

More than 11 million Latinos voted in the 2012 presidential election. However much impressive, it still means that 2.6 million Latinos who were registered did not vote. Close to 52 percent of an estimated 23 million Latinos who were entitled to cast their vote didn't do so. About 8.4 percent of the 2012 voting electorate was made up of Latino voters. This share is higher than 2008, which is an increase of 1.5

million voters. Evaluations show that the republican presidential nominee must gain the support of 47 percent to 52 percent of Latino voters in order to win the general election in 2016.[30]

6. Immigration is a top issue of concern among Latino voters

According to Polling; it clearly shows that immigration is the key issue for Latino voters, with wide support for comprehensive immigration reform, a pathway to citizenship and implementation of the recent administrative actions. Right next to the two top issues of concern, which are the economy and education, immigration comes in significantly ahead.

According to a new Pew Research Center analysis of the U.S. Census Bureau data, Hispanic millennials will account for nearly half of the record 27.3 million eligible voters projected for 2016, which is a share greater than any other racial or ethnic group of voters. A reflection of the large track of Latino millennial eligible voters shows the gigantic importance of youth in the U.S.-born Latino population and as a source of Latino eligible voter growth. According to Pew Research Center projections, between the period running from 2012 to 2016, close to 3.2 million out of the youthful U.S. citizen Latinos are going to grow to be adults and be able to form part of the population eligible to vote.[31]

Three election simulations conducted by CAP action for 2016 represented three different scenarios based on assumptions about party preferences.

Simulation 1: This first simulation undertakes that party preferences and voter turnout among all ethnic groups in 2016 will remain constant as it happened in 2012.[32] This is because 2012 elections generated relatively high provision for Democrats in comparison to other elections amid minority voters. This is usually the most favorable simulation for the potential Democratic contender.

Simulation 2: This simulation makes the assumption that all racial and ethnic groups' party preferences in 2016 will mirror results from 2004 when republicans revel in higher levels of support from minority voters.[33]

Simulation 3: This simulation takes the assumption that white voters in 2016 elections may vote with the similar party preferences as seen in 2012 while minority voters could vote according to their party preferences as was in 2004. This is because the 2004 election generated moderately high support among ethnic voters for Republicans and the 2012 election generated reasonably high support amongst white voters for Republican contenders.[34]

Each of the simulations was performed for each of the six states and key findings were that;

a) A democratic candidate will have a strong electoral advantage in 2016 if he or she is able to retain high levels of support from minority voters, especially Latino voters. Under stimulation one, where a Democratic candidate had the same kind of support from voters as witnessed in 2012 in every state but Arizona, and putting into consideration the demographic shift, it would be seen that Democrats increase the share of votes among five of the six states that were featured. These states are Florida, Nevada, New Mexico, Arizona, and Colorado. In New Mexico, Nevada, and California, the Democratic candidate would still receive more than 50 percent of the overall vote share and win the state's 66 electoral votes.

b) Demographic predictions give a basis that, Nevada is possibly going to become more and more hard for a Republican presidential aspirant to clinch the win. Also, a latent candidate who is a Republican may not be able to scoop the win in Nevada in any simulation mentioned, with the assumption that levels of turnout take a similar trend to that witnessed in 2012. In case a high level of support from ethnic voters is not maintained by Democrats, while Republicans reclaim their higher levels of support from minority voters in 2004 and higher support from the white from 2012, Republicans are likely to see the Presidential race in Nevada heighten in their favor.

c) The key swing state of Florida may be up for grabs but this depends on how political parties will be able to appeal and gain support from minority voters and in particular Latino voters. As done in simulation one, in case Democrats are capable of maintaining the same levels of support from voters as happened in 2012, the Democratic contender would win Florida along with its 27 electoral votes. As done in simulations two and three, if minority voters could have similar party preferences as it was in 2004, the Republican candidate could possibly win the state.

d) Moreover, white voters are still going to play critical roles in states of Colorado and Arizona. These two states may be experiencing fast demographic shifts, more than 7 in 10 votes will be cast by white voters in Colorado and Arizona in 2016. Another exceptional state is Colorado where white voters have moved away from Republican candidates rather than toward them. Simulations have indicated that the outcome of the election would be determined by whether white voters carry on trending towards Democrats or go back to support Republicans at 2004 levels.

Over the next decades, the increasing Latino population across the nation is going to exercise a greater electoral clout. In the 1980s, Latinos in the U.S. represented just 6.5 percent of the entire population in the nation. Today

Latinos have increased in population to represent about 17 percent of the U.S. population with such a trend, they are expected to account for approximately 29 percent by 2060.[35] Estimates of the probable threshold of support from Latino voters emphasize the significance of the Latino vote that Republicans would have to secure in order to win the presidential race. In the 2004 election, there was a projection that Republicans needed to capture about 40 percent of the Latino vote so that they win the presidency.

On the contrary, as the share of qualified Latino voters continues to increase, the share of whites that are eligible to vote has been dropping since the 1980's. In 1980s, whites represented 85 percent of all eligible voters, however, this has dipped to about 70 percent to date. By 2060, only about 40 percent of eligible voters are going to be white while Latinos will account for 27 percent. Though the Latino voters are going to be the largest share of eligible minority voters, on the other hand, it is important to understand that Asian and other eligible voter communities are also growing pretty fast from the 6 percent of eligible voters recorded in 1980 to anticipated 14 percent in 2060.[37]

Because of the large portion of eligible millennial voters, the Latino voter attendance rate could be lower than expected and the rising number of immigrant Latinos who are U.S. citizens may help improve the turnout rates of the Latino vote. In 2012, about 53.6 percent of immigrant Latinos cast their votes, a full 7.5 percentage points higher than the 46% majority voter turnout rate among U.S.-born Latinos that year.

Another reason why the Latinos may not vote in large numbers in relation to their population in the 2016 elections is that few states with large Hispanic populations are probably strategic battlegrounds. Candidates often focus their outreach efforts in these states in presidential elections, therefore, raising the chances that a voter may be contacted and possibly turn out to vote. Latino-rich states like California, Texas and New York, for example, are not likely to be presidential tossup states. Florida, Nevada, and Colorado are likely to once again be battleground states in the race for president. In each of the three, Hispanics make up more than 14 percent of eligible voters.

Latinos seemingly try to "punch below their weight" when it comes to elections because close to more than half of the nation's Latino population is either quite young to vote or doesn't hold U.S. citizenship. By comparison, just 20 percent of the nation's white population is not eligible to vote for the same reasons, as is 28 percent of the black population and 44 percent of the Asian population.

Arizona
In the previous four presidential elections, Arizona state voted for a Republican candidate. In the event that Democrats manage to retain increased support from minority voters, it is however likely that demographic

disparities in Arizona could slowly reduce the GOP grip on the state overtime. Since 1980, the population of racial and ethnic minority groups here has been growing quickly. While the whites made up 83 percent of the population in 1980, today they constitute about only 55 percent. On the contrary, the Latino population seems to have progressively increased from 13 percent in 1980 to 33 percent today. With the increasingly growing racial as well as ethnic minority population in this state, it means that the number of eligible minority voters is also correspondingly increasing. It has been projected that the share of eligible Latino voters in the state will grow from about 22.6 percent of all voters in 2012 to about 22.4 percent in 2016. Arizona may be deemed to be a majority-minority state come the year 2022, however, in regard to the 2016 election, it is likely that the white vote may continue to have a huge impact, especially if the attendance gap among Latinos take a similar trend to that of 2012.[38]

California

Since 1992, California has been voting for Democratic presidential candidates, and the Democratic edge of attaining victory has been gradually increasing year after year. The widening share of eligible minority voters within California implies that, in the event the minority voters keep on supporting Democrats at towering levels, then California is only going to become more well-established as a Democratic stronghold. Whites are expected to constitute less than 23 percent of the population of

California by 2060, while Latinos are going to account for 48 percent.

The increasing share of eligible minority voters within California implies that, if minority voters go on with the trend of supporting Democrats at increased levels, then California is going to be likely a reliable Democratic state. In the three simulations undertaken, Democrats are continuing to win the majority of the popular vote.

Colorado

Colorado is regarded as one of the swing states, and it gave votes to Republican candidate George W. Bush during the elections of 2000 and 2004. However, it flipped its support in the previous two presidential elections to give votes to a Democratic candidate. It is a shift of events that appears to have been contributed in part by Latino voters, which is the largest racial and ethnic minority population in this state. In case Democrats maintain strong support from Latino voters in addition to other minority voters together with the growing section of Latino voters, it is likely that Republicans may have a difficult time in retaking Colorado in 2016.

In Colorado, the population of racial and ethnic minority groups has been increasing since 1980. Latino populace has briskly increased from 9 percent in 1980 to about 22 percent in 2014, and is anticipated that it will reach about 40 percent by the year 2060. In spite of the demographic shifts, Colorado like Arizona, continue to have predominantly white electorate.

During the 2012 elections, whites represented about four in five equivalent to about 78 percent of entire votes. Similarly, in 2016, whites are still expected to cast more than three in four, equivalent of 76 percent votes.[39] Grippingly though, Colorado is one state in which Republican candidates have been shifted away from by white voters overtime. In the event that Democrats manage to retain a big support from minority voters in 2016, and in this case the largest share being Latino voters as it were 2012, it means Democrats may have a bigger margin of victory in the 2016 elections. As shown under stimulation 1, Democrats are likely to increase their edge of victory by about 1 percentage point; that's from 51 percent in 2012 elections to 52.1 percent in 2016 elections. Nonetheless, as it were in 2004, if minority voters are able to support a Republican contender at higher stages, then Republicans may regain Colorado in 2016.

Florida
This is a state that has been a powerful swing state in regard to presidential politics. From 1976, there has been a peculiar trend; the candidate who has clinched the win in this state has eventually managed to taken the White House in all except one instance, and this is when George W. Bush scooped the win of Florida in 1992 but went to lose the election to Democrat candidate Bill Clinton.

During the 2016 elections, the 29 electoral votes of Florida are going to make the state nearly essential for any viable electoral pathway to the Oval Office.

There has been a changing electoral landscape in Florida owing to the increasing advancing racial and ethnic minority population. In 1980, a 4 percentage population of eligible voters in the state was Latino voters. In Florida the number of Latino electorate is projected to increase to 18.2 percent by 2016, which is an increase by 1.6 percentage points recorded in 1980. Meanwhile, the white electorate nose-dived from 81 percent of eligible voters recorded in 1980 to about 66.7 percent in 2012.

A downward trend is expected to continue meaning the number will go down further by 2016.[40] There has been a change in party inclination amongst Latino voters and this is seen to have been a key contributor in swinging Florida state to president Obama in the previous two elections of 2008 and 2012.

Latino voters favored Republican George Bush in 2004 being up by a 12-point margin, that's 56 percent to 44 percent. However, the numbers upturned in 2012, considering that 60 percent of Latino voters chose to vote for president Obama. Therefore, voting proclivity among Florida Latinos is consider a vital electoral driver, which in turn affects the results of presidential election.

New Mexico

In five of the last six presidential elections, New Mexico has given its votes to Democratic candidates, except for in 2004 when Republican candidate George W. Bush was given Florida's five electoral votes. One thing about New Mexico is that it is quite unique among the six states that are analyzed here. Its electorate makes up the biggest fraction of non-white voters of any U.S. state other than the District of Columbia and Hawaii.

During the 2012 elections, non-white voters constituted 49 percent of the entire votes cast in presidential election. Latinos on the other hand made up 37 percent of voter population. The eligible voter population in New Mexico is majority-minority, where white's eligible voters make up only about 46 percent. [41] At the same time, the Latino share of electorate is expected to move to the same level as the share of white voters, rising by 1.7 percentage points from 2012 elections to reach 42.3 percent in 2016.

Nevada

Nevada is an essential swing state; since 1980, it has voted with the victor in each presidential election. In 2016, it will play an important role in the presidential election. As the simulations demonstrate, the demographic changes in the state (characterized by increased Latino voters and a huge support of Democrats by Latinos) will ultimately make it difficult although not impossible, for Republicans to clinch the win in 2016.

In 1980, the Latino share of the entire Nevada's population was 6 percent, and this had almost tripled to 26 percent in 2012. The size of the Latino eligible voters has really boomed in this state almost tripling from 5 percent to reach 16.8 percent in 2012.

Other minority voters in Nevada are also expected to rise. Latinos not only casting more votes in Nevada, but also preferring Democratic candidates. In 2004, about 60 percent of Latinos voted for Secretary Kerry, a Democratic contender, whereas close to 39 percent opted for George Bush, the Republican candidate. [42]

It is becoming a tall order for Republicans to win in this state as indicated by the election simulations, but this does not mean that it is impossible for Republicans to clinch the win. None of the simulations carried out showed any possibilities for a Republican winning in 2016.

From the election of 2012, analysts cited the heightening power of Latino vote. Projected changes and turn of events may result in dramatic electoral consequences. For example, there is an increasing population of Latinos that are turning 18 every year. Also, there are more legal permanent residents who are establishing themselves. Many eligible Latinos are now registering to vote. On top of that, surplus Latino voters are turning out to cast their vote. Such changes clearly show that at present Latinos are a growing segment of the eligible voters meaning that there is a potential for them to gain more political power in the elections of 2016 and beyond.

Election candidates from both sides of the aisle are likely to benefit if they understand the electoral and political power that is being unleashed by the Latino population.

How Latinos are powering the U.S. economy

In an interview with Luis Peña, a good friend and renowned restaurateur and serial entrepreneur, we discussed the role Latinos and Latino immigrants in the US economy. Luis Peña also happens to own two of the best restaurants in San Diego, one of them a tribute to the migrant worker bearing the name Bracero, for the migrant worker program. Upon entering his Bracero restaurant you'll see black and white photos of Braceros, sculptures dedicated to agriculture and the history of the farm hands spread all along the walls.

Luis, an immigrant himself, employs over one hundred people of all ages and all ethnic backgrounds. He agrees Latinos are sparking new businesses all across the country. "If you're risking your life to come here, opening a business doesn't seem like a big risk" he says with a smile. Many people see Hispanics as hard working employees, they don't realize they're also the backbone of the growing economy.

We took the conversation to social issues and Obamacare. Being an entrepreneur, I thought Luis would be against it. "I'm glad my employees have healthcare and they are too. We forget we're not just here to make money, I'm responsible for more than one hundred families" he said. This brings another point. Latinos are not only entrepreneurs, they are social entrepreneurs, caring about their employee's family, education, and health.

Since 2000, the Hispanic population in the United States has immensely contributed to the population growth of the country. Analyzing and understanding the implication of the Latino population in the U.S. and it's grown over the years offers a clear picture of what to expect from this ethnic group in economic and political spheres within the U.S. In the historical population growth of U.S. Hispanics, there has been notable trends. The period after 2000 has seen an increased rate of growth of the population reaching a record 55. 4 million as per the U.S. Census Bureau data of 2014. By 2016, it had been predicted that there will be about 58.1 million Hispanics in the USA.[43]

In 1850, Hispanics in the U.S. were about 117,000. In 1900, the population had reached 500,000 while in 1950, it reached 3.2 million. By 2000, the Hispanics had grown to reach a population of 35.3 million people. In 2010, according to the U.S. Census Bureau, Hispanics were estimated to be 50.5 million people. A recent population census conducted in 2014 showed that the U.S. Hispanic population has grown to 55.4 million people representing about 17.4 percent of the U.S. total population. This was an increase of about 1.2 million or 2.1 percent from the previous year 2013.[44] However, statistics indicate that a slower growth is being experienced among the Hispanic population in U.S. today than began in the year 2010. Part of the reason why there has been a slowed population growth of Hispanics in the U.S. is because of the slowdown in immigration in recent years from Latin American and specifically from Mexico.

The 2016 presidential elections may be focusing on immigrants as they form a big share of the U.S. national population and the eligible registered voters. However, candidates seeking for support to clinch local, state, and national seats need to know how Latinos influence the economy and the national policy changes. Latinos are a huge driver of U.S. economic growth. Those on the campaign trail or even the media may not have an idea on how Latinos contribute to the economy; unless you own or run a retail business, then you might not understand what this means. Much of the efforts on the campaign trail and media talks have concentrated on getting past immigration forgetting the extent to which Latinos do power the American economy.

The purchasing power of the Latinos has been growing at least by 70 percent faster when compared to Americans as a whole from the late 1980s.[45] In 2014, Latinos contributed about 33 percent of Nissan to 100 percent of Honda automakers' combined retail sales growth within the U.S., as reported by IHS Automotive's Polk Market data unit. The good thing is, U.S. consumer-products companies are aware of this and their leaders are focused on bringing in growth strategies that revolve around the Latino consumers.

Also, Latinos in the U.S. make up a larger young population than Americans as a whole. This young population is key in driving the workforce of the U.S. On top of that, young Latinos in the U.S., are becoming better educated and earning more than ever. What this means is that the Latino household formation is also rising.

Latinos are also driving the wheel of new-business formations in the nation, according to a study conducted by Stanford Latino Entrepreneurship Initiative. From that study, the net new-business formations for Latinos increased by 47 percent from 2007 to 2012, while in the same period, the net new-business formations for non-Latinos declined by about 2 percent. [46] With new businesses, it also means new jobs. U.S. may not suffer a demographic crisis like that witnessed in Europe as the baby boomers retire because the young Latinos are going to take the position of these retiring Americans. The young Latinos are stepping into workplaces and paying taxes that will continue keeping the fiscal house of the nation in check.

The 2016 presidential campaign may have first unfolded as a disappointment from different sediments echoed to Latino populations in the U.S., and especially those of Mexican origin. As the campaigns for 2016 election moved on, there seems to be a real alarm. If presidential candidates and the U.S. voters are able to understand the truth of Latinos in driving U.S. economic growth, they would have a different approach in their campaigns to reach out to Latinos.

Instead of the campaigns dwelling on immigration and fears that immigrants are going to take up more jobs in the U.S., they should look to Latinos as a pillar of the nation's economy. There are strong but mistaken impressions about the U.S. Latinos, something that makes the community feel sidelined in issues pertaining to social, economic, and political dimensions.

Latino Influence by State

A List of the Latino Population By State

Below is a list of states and their Hispanic demographic share as per the data of 2011. The figures may however have changed as of 2016. However, these show how the population is distributed in various states and how it is likely to affect the results of the 2016 election and future presidential elections.

- California— has 14,358,000 Hispanic population taking up a share of 38 percent of the state's entire population
- Texas— has 9,794,000 Hispanic populations with a 38 percent share of the population of the state
- Arizona- there is 1,950,000 Hispanics in this state taking up a share of about 30 percent of entire population
- Florida— of the Florida's population, Hispanics take a share of 23 percent with a population of 4,354,000 people
- New York— hosts more than 3,497,000 Hispanics representing 18 percent of the state's population
- New Mexico— has about 972,000 Hispanics who represent close to 47 percent of the entire population in that state
- Nevada— in this state, Hispanics represent 27 percent of the population number with 738,000 people
- Colorado— has a Hispanic population of 1,071,000 which accounts for about 21 percent of the entire state's population
- Illinois— consists of a Hispanic population of 2,078,000 taking a share of 16 percent of the state's population

- New Jersey— has a 1,599,000 Hispanics who account for close to 18 percent of the population
- Connecticut— hosts more than 494,000 Hispanics representing 14 percent of the state's population.[47]

Mapping the Latino Electorate by Congressional District
(A list of the largest trends for Latinos)[48]

More than 27.3 million U.S. Latinos are eligible to vote during the 2016 presidential elections. The list below is of Congressional Districts with the largest Hispanic eligible voter population.

Congressional Districts	Hispanics Eligible voters
Arizona Congressional District 2	113,000
Arizona Congressional District 1	90,000
Arizona Congressional District 3	235,000
Arizona Congressional District 7	181,000
Arizona Congressional District 9	91,000
California Congressional District 6	102,000
California Congressional District 8	142,000
California Congressional District 9	121,000
California Congressional District 10	136,000
California Congressional District 16	177,000
California Congressional District 19	144,000
California Congressional District 20	143,000
California Congressional District 21	206,000

California Congressional District 22 167,000
California Congressional District 23 143,000
California Congressional District 24 113,000
California Congressional District 25 132,000
California Congressional District 26 145,000
California Congressional District 27 120,000
California Congressional District 28 100,000
California Congressional District 29 216,000
California Congressional District 31 189,000
California Congressional District 32 245,000
California Congressional District 34 180,000
California Congressional District 35 255,000
California Congressional District 36 164,000
California Congressional District 37 121,000
California Congressional District 38 260,000
California Congressional District 39 130,000
California Congressional District 40 239,000
California Congressional District 41 205,000
California Congressional District 42 141,000
California Congressional District 43 141,000
California Congressional District 44 214,000
California Congressional District 46 177,000
California Congressional District 47 114,000
California Congressional District 51 246,000
California Congressional District 53 140,000
Colorado Congressional District 1   101,000
Colorado Congressional District 7   106,000
Florida Congressional District 7   100,000
Florida Congressional District 9   212,000

Florida Congressional District 14	113,000
Florida Congressional District 23	167,000
Florida Congressional District 24	128,000
Florida Congressional District 25	266,000
Florida Congressional District 26	309,000
Florida Congressional District 27	301,000
Illinois Congressional District 3	113,000
Illinois Congressional District 4	211,000
Nevada Congressional District 1	106,000
New Jersey Congressional District 8	201,000
New Mexico Congressional District 9	143,000
New Mexico Congressional District 1	209,000
New Mexico Congressional District 2	211,000
New Mexico Congressional District 3	176,000
New York Congressional District 7	162,000
New York Congressional District 13	225,000
New York Congressional District 14	160,000
New York Congressional District 15	241,000
Texas Congressional District 2	95,000
Texas Congressional District 11	152,000
Texas Congressional District 15	297,000
Texas Congressional District 16	324,000
Texas Congressional District 18	110,000
Texas Congressional District 19	142,000
Texas Congressional District 20	315,000
Texas Congressional District 21	140,000
Texas Congressional District 23	275,000
Texas Congressional District 27	230,000
Texas Congressional District 28	272,000

Texas Congressional District 9	213,000
Texas Congressional District 30	100,000
Texas Congressional District 33	145,000
Texas Congressional District 34	314,000
Texas Congressional District 35	239,000

The above list shows the key areas with higher Hispanic eligible populations. These areas are in states that are regarded as the battlegrounds for the Hispanic votes in the U.S. By presidential candidates putting efforts to win the support of Latinos in these areas, they increase their odds of clinching the lead.

The Latino Electorate by State
(A list of the largest states and the number of electoral votes for 2016) [49]

State	Latino eligible voters
Texas	28.1 percent
New Mexico	40.4 percent
Arizona	21.5 percent
California	28.0 percent
Florida	18.1 percent
Colorado	14.5 percent
Illinois	10.5 percent
New York	13.8 percent
Nevada	17.2 percent

List of the Number of Congress Positions for The Largest Latino States [50]

State	Number of Congress positions	
Texas	36	(25 are Republicans)
New Mexico	3	(2 are Republicans)
Arizona	9	(5 are Republicans)
California	53	(14 are Republicans)
Florida	27	(17 are Republicans)
Colorado	7	(4 are Republicans)
Illinois	18	(8 are Republicans)
New York	27	(9 are Republicans)
Nevada	4	(3 are Republicans)

While it may be said that not all Hispanics have the same feelings about any given issues, on the other hand, there are some issues that stand out and tend to grab the attention of Hispanic voters to Candidates affiliated with the Democratic Party. Issues like health care, immigration reforms, the economy, education, and criminal justice have been of concern among the Latino population. Since Democratic platforms try to address these issues, candidates who affiliate themselves with this Party are likely to win the support by the Hispanics. Having more Republicans in Congress would mean that the push for changes in laws that touch on these sensitive issues cited by the Latino community is strengthened.

History of Latinos in Politics

Hispanics play a huge impactful role in national politics. Nevertheless, how they turn out is a key factor in determining which party will take control of the White House and Congress. Being the largest minority group in the U.S., the Hispanics comprise about 17% of the entire population, according to the United States Census Bureau. This number is expected to grow with time and with this growth, the Hispanic voters turn out in larger numbers. Therefore, both Democrats and Republicans are trying to appeal to these groups across the country. Although Democrats are likely to be more favored by the Hispanic voters, Republicans may still have an opportunity to change the odds.

Latinos make up the largest ethnic minority group in the United States. Back in 1990, Hispanics population was 22 million, or roughly 9% of the total population. In the year 2000, their population grew to 35 million and in 2010, their population increased to 51 million, which is approximately 13% of the total population. Typically, around one million Hispanic people are added to the American population every year. By 2013, Hispanics population grew to 54 million, or 17% of the total population. In addition, recent studies estimate that by 2060, the number of Hispanics will account for about 31% of the total population.[51]

The state of New Mexico accommodates the largest group of Hispanic people (47% of the total population) followed by California, with 38%. They are also greatly represented in Texas (38%) and Florida (23%). In addition, Colorado, Arizona, Illinois, New Jersey and New York all have more than 16%.

Recent voting trends show that Hispanics make up a significant block of the American voters, and that their population is likely to grow. In 2010, Hispanics constituted 7% of all voters in Federal elections, but by 2012, they amounted to 8%. However, fewer Hispanic Americans are registered to vote compared to black or white Americans. Following the 2013 data from Gallup, only 51% of all qualified Hispanic citizens were registered to vote in the 2012 Federal elections. At the same time, 60% of Asian voters, 81% of black voters and 85% of white voters were registered. The 2014 midterm elections held similar numbers: 25 million Hispanics were fit to vote, but the actual number of Hispanic voters was even worse than the already low countrywide turnout of 37%.

Although not all eligible Latinos are actually voting, they still boost the general minority vote. Therefore, the American electorate suggests that a collective ethnic minorities' voting preferences can change the outcome of presidential elections, taking into account the deteriorating number of white voters.

Countrywide, the number of eligible Hispanic voter's amount to roughly 40% in New Mexico, 27% in Texas, 29% in California, 20% in Arizona, 17% in Florida, 15% in Nevada, 13% in New York, 12% in New Jersey, and 10% in Connecticut. Again, the voter turnout during the midterm elections was lower compared to other ethnic groups nationwide. A good example is the state of Florida. Here, only 36% of Hispanic voters went to vote in the 2014 midterm elections, while the overall turnout was 50%. However, despite the low turnout, Hispanic voters have the potential to strongly affect American elections.

The big question is; why is the Hispanic voter turnout low?

There are various important factors to consider. The small voter registration numbers among Latinos can be partly explained by the fact that most Latinos are not American born citizens. About six out of ten Hispanic voters (around 35%) were born in the United States, but 75% of American born Latinos registered to vote during the 2012 Federal elections. Those that are not citizens by birth registered at a much lower rate of 31%.

Some Hispanics are not fit to vote due to their immigration status. Latinos who are permanent residents but have not secured citizenship are permitted to vote in some local and state elections, but are prohibited from contributing in federal elections. Potential candidates for office are sometimes blamed for the low turnout rates, as they may not offer widespread platforms that include issues that are important to minority voters.

Historically, specific states in the United States have always voted for either Republicans or Democrats, whereas there are some states that swing back and forth between both parties, usually referred to as the 'swing states'. Often, presidential candidates take more time to campaign in such states, as they usually decide elections. In the coming 2016 election, the states with huge Latino populations are already being seen as the states to win. Such states include Florida, Nevada, Colorado, and Virginia.

Florida has the largest number of Hispanics among the swing states at 23% of the total population. The Hispanic electorate made up 17% of total voters during the 2012 elections. With the large population of Cubans in Florida, Republicans get more of their votes as the Cubans have historically voted for the Republicans. However, more Hispanics in Florida have recently been leaning towards the Democratic Party.

Colorado is the state that has the second largest Latino population among the swing states. Historically, Colorado has been tremendously Republican, but recent demographic trends have altered the odds for the GOP. In the last two Federal elections, Hispanic constituencies significantly supported Obama over Romney and McCain, helping him to victory.

The voting conditions in Nevada are uncertain, as both Presidents Bush and Obama won the state votes twice. Obama was able to win Nevada largely since Hispanic voters constituted 14% of the total electorate. On the other hand, Obama did not get much support from the white voters in Nevada, leaving substantial chances for the Republican Party to take more non-Hispanic votes in Nevada.

Conventionally, Red state Texas has the potential to turn into a swing state. About 30% of its eligible voters are Latinos and as a result, experts trust that the Hispanic vote can make a big difference in Texas in the 2016 Federal elections.

Despite the fact that Latino populations in the so called swing states are more likely to vote for the Democrats, a huge number of non-Hispanic whites in such states are still prodigiously Republican, making it possible for the GOP to win by capturing more white votes. This shows that Hispanic voters can play a significant pivotal role in the final voting decision, but may not be the deciding factor anywhere.

Not all Hispanics feel the same way about any given issue. Some support Republicans, but the bulk of Hispanics support the Democrats. There are particular issues that stand out and tend to draw the attention of Hispanics to cast their votes to Democratic candidates. Another thing is that Hispanic voters' views on primary issues like health care, immigration reform, the economy and education tend to align closely with Democratic platforms.

The traditional Republican attitude on immigration is the main reason why they seem to be less popular in the Hispanic communities than Democrats. The Democrats tend to give full support the comprehensive reforms pertaining to this issue of immigration. The 2014 national survey of Latinos discovered that 66% of registered Latino voters considered comprehensive immigration legislation a very important and urgent matter.

Usually, laws that are Republican-sponsored concerning immigration do not resonate well with Hispanic communities. A good example is the proposition 187 in California, which permitted law enforcement to search for undocumented immigrants and turn them in to immigration authorities. This is sometimes seen as the end of Red California, as the resulting controversy led to several Democratic victories. However, the 2014 national survey of Latinos revealed that 54% of registered Latino voters said that immigration is not the only factor that influences their voting decision in a candidate's position. Job creation and the economy were seen as more important issues, including healthcare.

Around one in five members of White House and Senate are an ethnic minority, which makes the 114th Congress the most diverse in the history of the United States. However, Congress remains unreasonably white when compared to the U.S. population, which has increasingly grown diverse in the recent decades.

Overall, non-whites (including Hispanics, blacks and Native-Americans) make up 17% of the new Congress, but this is still below these groups' 38% share of the country's population. This difference is also evident among the newly elected members of congress, since minorities comprise of 15% of new members of the House and Senate.

Diversity among the members of Congress has been growing for decades. However, the country's population has diversified even more quickly. Back when the 107th Congress took over in the year 2001, minorities were 12% of Congress, compared to about 31% of the country's population. In 1981, 6% of Congress was minority (Hispanic, Black, Asian or Native-American), while in the national population around 20% were non-white.

Among the minority groups, the largest growth has been among the Hispanics. In 2001, there were only 19 Hispanics in Congress, compared to the 32 Hispanics in Congress today. The rising number of minorities in Congress is mostly due to membership changes within the

House, where 20% of members are considered non-white, based on a report by CQ Roll Call. In 2001, the House had 60 minority seats. In the Senate, by comparison, only six out of a hundred senators belong to an ethnic or racial minority group, up from three senators in 2001.

The rise in minority numbers in the House from 2001 is considered to have largely come among newly elected Democrats, although Republicans also made some gains. Since 2001, the number of minority House Democrats increased from 56 to 74 now. Nevertheless, in spite of these non-white gains, white people make up 83% of the new Congress but only 62% of the population.

The choice of appointing John Perez succeed as the new speaker of California's state assembly later this month has been addressed as something of a breakthrough. The reason behind this is not that he is of Hispanic origin, but because he is openly gay. Kevin Deleon, who was Perez's competitor for the post is also Hispanic, as are many of Perez's predecessors including his cousin, Antonio Villargosa, who is currently the mayor of the city of Los Angeles. The weight of Hispanics in the political affairs of states such as Texas and California (where Mexican American Legislative Caucus entitles 44 of the 150 members of the state house of representatives) is now understood to be not only large, but also normal.

This year, the decennial census will confirm the enormous growth of Hispanics population. This influence will be both normal and evident in more parts of the country. The executive director of the National Association of Latino Elected and Appointed Officials (NALEO) known as Arturo Vargas, estimates that about one million Hispanics were omitted in the statistics during the last census. He claims that if one lives on somebody's couch or in a garage, as many Latinos do, it is quite easy not to be counted. This time around, there is an intensive effort to change that. If Census Bureau estimates are validated, about 16% of America's population will be seen to be Hispanic (since the label denotes to ethnicity and not race, anyone who describes themselves as Hispanic is deemed to be so).

According to William Frey of the Brookings Institution, latinisation is the most important democratic change in the United States, along with the maturing of baby-boomers. Hispanics account for half of America's total population growth since 2000, William Frey notes. According to him, to see America's future, we should look to its cities and its youth. White children are by now minorities in 31 of America's 100 largest metropolitan areas. For the United States as a whole, white children will become minorities in preschools by 2021 and in the general population by 2042. One result of this is the increase of Hispanic officials and politicians. Mr. Vargas counts close to more than 6000 in the country, mostly on the board of schools and utility districts as well as other branches of the local government that are "the first rung in the political ladder." There are also two Hispanic cabinet ministers, 26 Hispanic representatives and a Hispanic senator. In addition, New Mexico's governor is Latino. Since Sonia Sotomayor became Justice of the Supreme Court, "there is only one office that eluded us" Mr. Vargas says.

Paul Taylor, the director of the pew Hispanic center says that Hispanics have so far pressed below their weight in American politics, in contrast to blacks, who have pressed above theirs. Several Hispanics are undocumented immigrants, many others are too young to vote and others have simply not bothered. Mr. Frey describes Latinos as "notorious for not getting organized," as many consider themselves Guatemalan, Mexican, Salvadorian or Puerto Rican, rather than Hispanics. This resulted in Latinos being weaker as a block than blacks have been recently, or that the Irish were after the immigration wave during the 19th century. This may partially explain the reason why Texas has never had a Hispanic governor, and California has had only one, back in the 1830s.

All this however, is changing. It is well known that Latinos tend to respond more to anger and fear. During the 1990s in California, Hispanics are said to have read the seemingly anti-immigrant rhetoric of Pete Wilson who was a governor in the Republican Party, as racist and were annoyed when Californian voters passed a ballot measure aimed at barring undocumented immigrants from things like non-emergency public health care, education and welfare. Hispanics from California counteracted by fighting at the ballot box where they were registering in huge numbers, as Monica Lozano, who is a third generation Mexican as well as a publisher of LA Opinion recalls.

In future elections, Latinos are likely to be the centerpiece of election, or the 'kingmaker,' says Samuel Rodriguez, a pastor as well as the president of the national Hispanic Christian leadership conference, an evangelical association. They will be able to incline the electoral balance and turn many red or possibly blue-states to purple. This is because Latinos are ideal independents.

Hispanics tend to place family and faith at the epicenter of their lives, and are thus conservative on several social issues, from abortion to gay marriage. However, the same values incline them in contrast to white evangelicals and to communitarian economic policies normally considered liberal. In California, as renters rather than homeowners, Hispanics tend to be against proposition 13, a law that covers property taxes, and instead tries to favor taxes that pay for better education.

Marketing to Latinos

My good friend Miguel Contreras was holding an open house event and one of the gentlemen there he thought was a potential prospect actually was a friend of the homeowner. They walked into the house and started hanging out. Miguel was finalizing his day and getting ready to close the house. Contreras started a conversation with the gentleman who was in his early seventies, and they both got into a politics discussion. The gentleman was fascinated with what Miguel's political views and proceeded to ask him "Miguel, what's your nationality?"

Miguel stopped and greened for a second, "Wow! If you are asking my nationality then I am an American, because I was born and raised here, but what I think you are asking me is what my ethnicity is… is that correct?" Then the gentleman said, "Oh, yeah!"

So, Miguel told him, "If you're looking for my ethnicity, then it is Mexican American. I am of Mexican origin but born and raised in the United States."

The older gentleman shook Contreras's hand and said, "Oh my God, I'm impressed with your knowledge about that… it's interesting you are taking it that way."

Miguel proceeded to ask the gentleman what was so impressive about that and he said, "Oh, you know, most Hispanic people say they're Mexican. I never know if they were born in Mexico and immigrated or if they just want to be Mexican because their parents are Mexican."

The gentleman continued to say, "But yours is very impressing... I'm really blown away by your response." Miguel continued conversing, "It is always interesting that 'Anglo-Americans' always ask what my nationality is because they know what my name is — 'Miguel Contreras.' They must still ask what my nationally is... they assume that for some reason, I am not from this country." This is something that was off putting to Miguel, but then that is the question he gets often. My friend knows what nationality means and what ethnicity means.

The interesting part is that the gentleman was aware that Miguel was educated and he was indeed surprised. This older gentleman was equally surprised too to find that Miguel was of Mexican descent because he was a fair skinned guy with blue eyes. "So, is your family originally from Spain?" the gentleman continued. Miguel gets that question often and to him it's laughable. Miguel said, "I don't know, maybe 200 years ago."

When someone asks you about your nationality, it's like they don't understand. This is a two-part question based on how they reply to such a question.

Miguel thinks that when we talk about nationality and ethnicity, because of shared ignorance, some people may not say what they mean. They use the word nationality interchangeably with heritage.

If people ask you, "Are you from Spain?" Does that mean they are asking you why you aren't brown and a gardener?

Miguel said that people choose to see what they want often times, what is portrayed in the media. There is more to do with image and color that tends to raise the question, "Are you from certain part of the world?"

From this conversation, it shows how 'Anglo-Americans' perceive Latino community in U.S. and it gives some insight on how misunderstood the community is by the 'Americans'.

Failing to understand and connect with the Latinos makes it difficult for politicians and political campaigners to lure them to vote for them.

Campaigning to Latinos Starts with the First Marketing Rule: Know Your Market!

I often speak at conferences and other public events about how to market to Latinos and always start by asking the company or the audience questions such as: Who's your target market? What is the action you would like them to do? How do you follow up? All standard marketing questions.

To the first question, the answer is "We would like to target Latinos". I expect such an answer, however it's not the specific answer. In marketing, you need to know everything about your client. Men or women, annual salary, education, kids, age, where they live, their values, etc.

It's not the same to target a Latino with a $75,000 car over one with a $11,000 one. Here I can already see the questions on the faces of the executives. They know this information, they use it every day to segment their market, however they thought Latinos were the segment. No, they are how you start it, then you need to ask all the other usual marketing questions to get to your answer. Again, my clients had in their mind that Latino meant the construction worker or the maid, not the doctor or the lawyer making $250,000 per year.

These simple segmentation questions leave my clients wondering how they'll target the Latino consumer as I continue with questions:
- Are they first generation immigrants? Second, Third? Fourth?
- Do they speak fluent Spanish?
- Do they watch TV in Spanish, English or both?
- Do they watch CNN or Univision for news?

- Do they watch soccer? Which league, Mexican, Spanish, All Europe?
- Do they prefer to listen to the game in English or Spanish?

In politics, influencing people to vote for you or your candidate requires that you understand them and market yourself the right way. It may be similar to the way you market products to consumers, but it is a little different in the sense that there is no single political campaigner. For example, you may have a particular political campaigner for the Republican Party this time, and next time you have a different one. In the U.S., a campaign manager will work for a candidate or a candidate will hire a campaign manager, sometimes the same one for every election and other times a different one. We still have many people running for presidency, and we had a lot when we started the 2016 presidential election, especially in the side of Republicans- each with different points of view, different marketing strategy, and a different way of seeing the Latino population. These campaign managers relied on different people to tell them about the Latino population. This is not the way you market.

The perfect way would require that each party have an expert and that expert would be a Latino, or of Latino parents, or of Latino grandparents. The expert should also know more about the culture of the Latinos. That person would know what the Latino thinks. He would know everything about the Latino the same way a marketing professional knows about his or her avatars or customers.

The campaign manager should not just know about where Latinos live, how much they earn, but also things or issues that worry them the most. He or she would need to know if Latinos sleep or why they don't sleep well— meaning what really troubles them. The campaigner would want to know what are the top five most important things to Latinos.

The campaigner should know the demographics, geography, and economic status of these people including where they live, how their population is distributed, what they earn, how many children they have, what their social values are, their religious affiliations, social norms, and how they perceive a family to be. The single most important thing is knowing how to make an emotional connection with the Latinos in the U.S. That is the holy grail of reaching and influencing the Latinos to vote for you.

The first thing you need to know is that if Latinos are worried that you're going to deport them or their family, then you're not establishing the right kind of emotional connection. On the contrary, you're establishing the wrong type of emotional connection with Latinos no matter what you try to do, as Lizet Ocampo of *the Center* for *American Progress Action Fund*, told me.

If you start your conversation with Latinos and say, "I want to deport your mother, or I want to deport your father, your aunt, your nephew, or your uncle, "then they will say, "I won't vote for you no matter what you say." And, this is what is happening especially with the right side of politics.

"If you start a conversation with these kinds of words, then as a Latina, I'm sorry, I will not vote for you." Lizet told me over our interview. "We are not connecting emotionally with Latinos. If you're going to deport my family or someone I know, then we cannot connect. Don't come to my house." Lizet knows of what she speaks. She's not only the Associate Director of Immigration for the Center for American Progress Action Fund, she also campaigned for president Obama on both campaigns before she pushed for immigration policy reform working in the White House. Daughter of immigrants who worked as field hands in California, she not only understands politics, and she also understands immigrants, campaigns, and policymaking.

Political candidates are changing the way they campaign every couple of years without learning and keeping experts around them to show them more about Latinos. It seems that political candidates are not listening to what Latinos want and this is bad for the candidates, the campaign managers, and Latinos.

In the next chapters, we'll look at why most things you know about Latinos are wrong. We will examine how

Latino immigrants (both documented and undocumented) are very important and how most Anglo-Americans don't know they have a Latino is next door. We will talk about how you can get to know Latinos by culture, food, language, and lifestyle.

You cannot connect with Latinos if you don't understand them. Even the labels we use are incorrect such as the words "Latino" and "Hispanic."

For people educated in Latin-America there's only one continent. Yes, the American continent. That's the way I learned it in school. I went to school in Mexico up to high school, and was taught there are five continents. If this is right, where did the word Latinamerica, Latinoamerica or Latin-America come from?

Latin-America was a word used to describe Latinos from the American Continent and distinguish them from Latinos from Europe. Latinos being the peoples who speak romance languages, or of Roman roots. Latinos include the people form America who speak Spanish and Portuguese, plus those of Italy, Spain, France, and Portugal.

Who is the modern Latino? That word used in the USA to refer to those peoples of Latin-American descent? The ethnicity behind the Latin-Americans and the US Latino includes cultures and ethnicities from Rome, Arabia, Africa, Portugal, Indigenous Americans, and many more.

We'll surely explore more about ethnicity in this book. Without knowing were Latinos come from it is impossible to understand them and influence them in any way, this includes the goal of getting their long term political affiliation.

Private Planes and Your Mexican Next Door

Your Mexican Next Door

I went to the medical clinic with a sore throat during one of my trips to Texas. I had to give a presentation the next day and wanted to make sure I didn't have a contagious infection. After I checked in at the front desk, the nurse took me to a cubical where she took my temperature and blood pressure.

"Let me take you to a room. The doctor will be here soon," said the nurse.

I followed her to a small room where I waited for the doctor. A blond man entered the room in a white lab coat. He was about six feet four inches tall with dirty blond hair and light blue eyes accompanied by an elongated smile.

"Hello Mr. Olson, I see your throat is bothering you today." He told me with a slight Texan accent. His lab coat had Dr. Schmitz embroidered over the pocket.

"Please call me Jorge. I'm way too young to be a mister," I said.

He clearly deduced that I spoke Spanish based on my pronunciation of my first name.
"Mucho gusto, Arturo Schmitz," (Good to meet you, Arturo Schmitz) he said in perfect Spanish.

I was taken aback. I didn't expect him to speak Spanish, especially with a perfect Mexican accent. I didn't expect his name to be Arturo either.

"Where are you from Arturo?" I asked continuing the conversation in Spanish.

"I'm from Mexico City," he said. "I moved to Texas and revalidated my medical degree a few years ago."

This is an example of what I call "Your Mexican Next Door". What I mean by this is that there are some Latinos, Mexican and others from other countries, that you don't even know speak Spanish or are from Mexico if you don't ask or listen to them speak in their native language. Yes, Schmitz is a Jewish name. Latinos have many different ethnicities, religions, and bloodlines.

Who is your Latino next door? This is probably a light-skinned family living in an all-white neighborhood. The wife is a doctor and the husband an executive in a large corporation or an entrepreneur. They're the life of the party at neighbor's reunions; they go to company outings taking the entire family along. Two blond girls with superior manners.

One day the neighbor hears Dr. Schmitz telling his daughters "En Español" (Say it in Spanish) a normal issue among white collar Latinos to make sure their children dominate both languages. The neighbor walks over and asks, "Do you speak Spanish?"

The man stares at the neighbor confused. "Of course I speak Spanish. I'm Mexican," he says. "Mexican?" the neighbor thinks. It doesn't make any sense. He's blonde, his daughters are blond, she has no accent, and he's a doctor. What's going on?

Your Latino next door, that's what's going on!

Private Planes

Thomas was cleaning his plane at a small airport in San Diego, California. It's a small one-engine plane he flies on the weekends. He even works on it once in a while as he is a professor of aeronautics at the local university. As he scrubs his plane with care, a gentleman passes by walking towards the local watering hole located a few yards away.

"When you're done can you do mine next?" he asks the man. "Sure thing boss," Thomas responded.

Ten minutes later Thomas enters the local bar to sit with friends. He sends a beer to the other man who asked him to clean his airplane. The man stares at him confused.

"Cheers," Thomas said while lifting his beer from across the bar and smiles in good cheer. The other man remains confused. He explained to his own friends what happened. They laugh. "He's the president of the aeronautics association," they explain. "He has a PhD and teaches at the university," they tell him. He blushes and walks over to apologize.

"There is nothing to apologize for," Thomas says. "I'm five-foot-tall and dark as night, you're not the first one to ask me to clean something," he says laughing.
This is a true story, one of many just from my friends and family without having to research the subject any further than my coffee table.

You can use the word "prejudice" however, if you do I want you to consider the social and neurological implications of that word. We touched on them before. The brain is trained to create patterns. Short dark man is a pattern, and the other gentlemen immediately thought of labor, not PhD.

What are the points of these stories? The point is stereotypes. Latinos are not all maids, gardeners or construction workers. They're not all dark skinned and short of stature. They come in all shapes, shades and professions. It's just that you may not recognize many of them on the street, or as your neighbors, because they don't fit the stereotype.

As a marketer, campaign manager or a political strategist, you need to understand the different shades of Latino culture. For starters, you have to understand Latinos, as we've said and will continue to say in the book. You then have to identify their believes, their goals, dreams, problems.

You have to inquire why many blue-collar workers lose the Spanish language after one generation. Consider how, on the other hand, white collar Latinos drill the Spanish language as if their life depended on it. Why the same segment sends their children to private school, even if they can only afford it with great sacrifice.

Before you understand the basics, you need to go back, way back, and become a colonization scholar. Latino values and beliefs start in Spain and other European countries that followed.

To understand and eventually influence Latinos, you need to follow branding and marketing rules. If the first rule is "Understand Your Market" The second rule is "Make an Emotional Connection". To do this, you have to learn what makes the population tick. Where are they coming from? Why do they cheer for their south of the border team and the USA team in the world cup!?

Overview of the Modern Latino World, the New World

Countries in Latin-America were conquered by Spain and Portugal. This is why in Brazil they speak Portuguese and the rest of the countries speak Spanish with the exception of a few small nations. The term Latin-America is said to have been coined in France under emperor Napoleon III. This was done as an effort to try to legitimize his claims of land in Mexico. Here is a list of Latin-America countries and the official and national languages they speak:

Brazil - Portuguese

Mexico - Spanish

Colombia -Spanish

Argentina - Spanish

Peru - Spanish, Quechua

Venezuela - Spanish and numerous indigenous dialects, about 40

Chile - Spanish

Ecuador- Spanish

Guatemala - Spanish 60% and Amerindian languages 40%
Cuba - Spanish
Haiti - French, Creole
Bolivia - Spanish, Quechua, Aymara
Dominican Republic - Spanish
Honduras - Spanish
Paraguay - Spanish, Guarani
Nicaragua - Spanish
El Salvador - Spanish
Costa Rica - Spanish
Panama - Spanish
Puerto Rico - Spanish, English

We have said that Latin America countries were conquered by Spaniards and Portuguese.

Notice the active words is "Conquered" and not "Colonized" or "Discovered". Spain landed in America and proceeded to first pelage, then enslave, rape, and exploit the population. This is after almost exterminating the majority of natives with war and disease.[52]

What do you know about the Spanish conquest? It was much different from the colonization that arrived from England. For starters, England sent families, Spain sent only men, at first, they were recruited from prison then followed by soldiers. This single fact changed the entire direction of the continent. One came to establish a family, the other to plunder.

The English colonists stayed away from the indigenous population at first, ignoring them for the most part. Spaniards plundered and enslaved natives immediately and almost whipped the culture completely. They ended up having to import 200,000 to 500,000[53] African slaves to substitute the now almost eradicated native population.

The history of the black race within Mexico seems to be both mysterious and illuminating. The story of Afro-Mexican become profound because of lack of documentation and the way the discussion of the subject is brought out.

Scholars have been conversant with the history touching on slavery in Mexico and in fact, even before the initial Spanish galleons come into existence, slavery was a common thing among various indigenous tribes within Mexico. In the real sense, it may be perceived that the Spanish were not the inventors of slavery, but then, they relied on it to be able to expand their empire and increase their wealth.

During the time the colonial period started in Mexico in the 16th and 17th centuries, the population of the indigenous people was annihilated by diseases. This created a labor shortage and to make up the scarcity, African slaves were taken to Mexico where they toiled in underground mines and sugar fields. African slaves were worth four times more compared to their indigenous Indian counterparts. They were highly prized because they had the physical endurance as well as stamina in the tropical climate characterized by hot sun.

Being subjected to dreadful conditions in the sugar plantations of Veracruz, the only viable option they had was to escape from the captors. Those who were successful in fleeing sought refuge in mountainous ranges sheltered by the jungle and canyons. Also, indigenous Indians fled to remote areas where they joined forces with the African slave escapees thereby forming families and communities.

An African slave by the name of Gaspar Yanga is said to have led an illustrious rebellion in Mexico in 1570. Yanga is believed to have been a member of the Africa's Gabon royal house making him a hero who led fellow slaves to have a successful revolt. Under the leadership of Yanga, the slaves were able to escape to the highlands of Veracruz. After almost thirty years of mountainous life, Yanga ultimately negotiated a treaty with Spaniards, but the treaty did not come easy. It was hard won and was only obtained following great hardship.

The town of Yanga in Veracruz stands as a living testimony and a symbol of the achievement of Yanga. It is not clear how many people were brought to Mexico as slaves, but some historians and scholars believe it was about 200,000 while others tally the number to be about 500,000. [52]

Colin A. Palmer, the Dodge Professor of History at Princeton University and also the Managing Editor for the Schomburg project, says that when he arrived in Mexico close to two decades ago to conduct research about the early history of Africans as well as their descendants there, surprisingly, he was told by a young student that he was going on a goose chase.

The young student told Palmer that Mexico did not import slaves from Africa and the people of African descent in the nation were just recent arrivals. There seems to be a lack of knowledge regarding African people in Mexico and this is something that has not changed much to date.

Palmer says that a short while ago, an engineer in Mexico who was of African descent told him adamantly that the blacks in the country were descendants of slaves who had escaped from Cuba and North America. The engineer proudly proclaimed that these fugitives had found sanctuary in what they called free Mexico.

However, when you examine the historical record, it brings out a different story. During the 16th century, Mexico, which was called New Spain during those days, possibly had more African slaves than most colonies in the Western Hemisphere. As early as the 1520s, Africans were slaves to the Spaniards. It is estimated that the slave trade ferried about 200,000 to 500,000 Africans to the colony during the approximately three hundred years it took place.

There are many blacks who were born in Mexico and who also found themselves becoming slaves. In 1829, the slavery institution was abolished by leaders of the new independent nation of Mexico.

To the Spanish colonists, African labor is believed to have been very important. In a time when indigenous people died of diseases or were killed, blacks are said to have assumed a lopsided portion of burden of work especially in those early colonial days. African slaves were used as laborers in the silver mines located at Taxco, Zacatecas, Pachuca, and Guanajuato. They also labored in sugar plantations of Morelos and Valle de Orizaba in the south.

African slaves were also used as laborers in textile factories of Oaxaca and Puebla as well as in households. Others worked on cattle ranches and in skilled trade. While the population of black slaves was not more than two percent, they made huge contributions to the colonial Mexico particularly during times when there was shortage of labor.

Slaves, wherever their population permitted, were able to create networks which allowed them to try to cope with the desperate situations they were going through. Through the networks, they could express their humanity and retain a sense of self. The networks were found in the port of

Veracruz, Mexico City, the sugar plantations, the major mining centers, and other key areas where slaves labored.

The networks allowed Africans to conserve and preserve a bit of their cultural heritage while also forging new and dynamic relationships. While the number of males was more than females, the slaves could find spouses from either their own or from other African ethic groups. Some other black slaves married or created amorous liaisons with indigenous people. To a small extent, they also married or created liaisons with Spaniards. During that time, a population made up of mixed bloods emerged and by the mid-18th century, there has a demographic ascendancy.

Like in many other parts of the Americas, the slavery witnessed in Mexico led to a severe physical as well as psychological price paid from the victims. There was abuse and resistance of oppression resulted in torture, whipping, mutilation, and being confined. The rate of deaths was quite high especially among the slaves who labored in silver mines and the sugar plantations.

Nonetheless, for the most part, they never broke their spirits, and at least many of them fled to find and establish settlements in remote areas. A group of slaves called "maroons" escaped to settle near Veracruz at the mountains. The slave owners saw these fugitives as a thorn to them. The colonist finally gave freedom to the intrepid Africans after failing to conquer them. These in turn were then allowed to build as well as administer their towns. In Mexico, Yanga is seen as a symbol of the black resistance even today.

In whichever form resistance took place whether escape or rebellion, it was perceived as an angry defiance of status quo or the desire of the slaves to reclaim their own lives. In this regard, black resistance takes a place in the revolutionary tradition of Mexico, and this is a tradition that has become a source of pride for a huge number of Mexicans.

Everywhere Africans lived in Mexico, they left imprints of their culture and genetics. Evidence of Africans ancestry is seen in states like Oaxaca, Guerrero, and Veracruz. These people see themselves as Mexicans yet their cultural heritage may not have entirely vanished. Some African traditions are carried in dance, music, songs, and other ways.

However, since the end of slavery, much has changed and in a constant changing society, it has become quite difficult for a minute minority to keep their traditions. While history has not been so kind to people of African descent in Mexico, they still remain to be productive among the society. It is only recently that studies on these groups of people were conducted including their contributions to Mexican society. Even as they become a shrinking population of the people of Mexico because of their ethnic blending into the population, contemporary black Mexicans are able to claim the proud legacy and they can draw strength from it, according to Colin A. Palmer.

The mix between Africans, Spaniards and the Indigenous population makes up much of modern Mexico. Each country in Latin America suffered the same fate by the Spanish conquest. As you travel through different parts of Mexico, Colombia, Cuba or Brazil you'll see eyes the deepest green and blue as you'll see of the lightest brown, grey and dark brown and if you're lucky, black. The same calls for skin color. You will encounter every shade and tonality and mix. One thing that you'll also notice is the lack of labels for many if the racial mixes. You don't see African-Mexicans, or Anglo-Cubans. You see Mexicans and Cubans. In my travels through Mexico the only very visible separation of classes and ethnicity has been of the Native Americans or Indigenous Population. Most of them where absorbed into the general population log ago, but there are still segregated groups all over Latin-America. They are generally of an agricultural society and maintain their language, food and other cultural traditions. I've seen firsthand how this segment of the population is treated, their land stolen, and their civil rights ignored. This, again is embedded into Latin-American heritage brought by ship form Spain.

The king of Spain declared the conquest and even genocide of Native Americans an act of god. The king, with the name Catholic in his title, Rey Catolico Fernando II, issued Las Leyes de Burgos (The laws of Burgos) in 1513. The now infamous El Requerimiento (The Requirement) Spanish law forces natives to convert to Christianity or be killed or enslaved. This at the time was a reaction to the human rights violations brought forward by the Monk Antonio de Montesinos.

In summary, The Requirement was supposed to be a good thing for the natives. Spain saw all of America as their land and all Americans as their property. At first during the conquest mass pillage took place, then it evolved into a very organized form of enslavement and exploitation both of natural resources and of its people.

Understanding and knowing the Latino voter is crucial for any political campaign strategy now and in the future. By understanding I mean you need to discover their background, where they come from, what their beliefs are and culture, their needs and their wants. By knowing, I'm referring to a personal emotional connection— a vested interest in their success as people, as a person, as a family.

In the next chapters, we'll explore the Latino cultures and beliefs so we can understand them better. What you do with that knowledge after the book, the "Knowing" part of the equation, is all up to you. For this, you have to reach out and make emotional connections with individuals and families.

Latinos, Hispanics and Mexican Americans

What is a Latino anyway?

The politically correct name at the moment seems to be Latinos. I remember not long ago it was Hispanics and before that Mexican Americans, but it excluded backgrounds from other countries so it's not used as much anymore. But what exactly is a Latino? Or a Hispanic now that we're exploring meanings?

The word Latino is most likely an abbreviation of Latinoamericano, or Latin-American. A person who speaks a romance language that had common roots in Latin, such as Portuguese in Brazil and Spanish in the rest of Latin-American.

The term Latinoamericano (Latinamerican) is descriptive of all the people living in America that speak a romance language. Used in comparison to people of Europe whose language also originates from Latin, such as it is in Italy, Spain, Portugal and France. It is interesting for me that Latin or Latino describes any Italian, Spaniard, French or Portuguese if used outside the USA.

It seems we have what I call a bad start. Even the label we give Latinos is not the best. If you sit down and speak with a Latino long enough and you ask them about their heritage they'll most likely tell you "I'm Mexican, or Puerto Rican, or Colombian" and proceed to tell you about their music, food, and customs. Calling everyone Latino would equal to calling Caucasians European instead of specifying the country where their ancestors came from. No longer would you hear "I'm Italian" or "I'm German", but I'm Caucasian European. It just don't have the same meaning.

The term Hispanic is actually a better evolution of the word to describe this segment of the population. Hispania is the Roman word used for the Iberian Peninsula, now Spain. Known as Hispania Romana, the empire claimed it as a territory for more than six hundred years.

Today, the word means "of Hispania" or "Of Spain", depicting the countries or people that come from a country that belonged to Spain. You can see how the name could be politically incorrect with many historians or politicians as it refers to the colonization and exploitation of the Native American population by Spain.

Latinos in the U.S. are a group forming the largest ethnic minority in the nation. American Latinos include groups like Mexican Americans who form the largest and oldest group, Cuban Americans, Puerto Ricans, Dominicans, and Central Americans from Nicaragua, El Salvador, and

Guatemala. The majority of Latino Americans found their way to the United States because of the various wars that existed for about 150 years.

Many Mexican Americans and Puerto Ricans are descendants of people whose homelands were seized by the United States. Many Mexicans, Central American and Cuban refugees fled from the revolutionary upheavals and civil wars, many of them funded by the USA. However, there are others who entered the U.S. with or without government visas trying to seek for economic opportunities.

The term Hispanic has been used to designate persons who reside in the U.S. whether legally or illegally and who are descendants of the aforementioned groups. The use of the label "Hispanic" has become as widespread as the groups themselves.

A Hispanic is a person in the United States bearing a Spanish surname and coming from Spanish speaking backgrounds. Nonetheless, many people prefer having other labels that reflect their place of origin, where they came from, where they live, or how they adapted to the dominant culture of U.S.

In essence, there are many Hispanics bearing broader subgroupings. These subgroups have wide spectrums of traditions and historical experiences. In order to understand the subgroups, it is important to appreciate the time, history, and place of these people. The label "Latino" is a generic term that was created by these people themselves and it signifies a varied and complex group of people.

There are certain things that are very crucial in Latino identities and they include location, demography, and linguistic affiliation.

Location helps determine the cultural roots of the U.S. Latinos before they moved to their present location. Most Mexican Americans occupy Southwest states of Texas, California, Arizona, New Mexico, and Colorado, which were part of northern Mexico before 1848. With a new influx of the population to other states like Illinois. Puerto Ricans coming from outside of the island settled in New York and some other large Midwestern cities. Cuban Americas are located in Florida, Dominicans in New York, and Central Americans in Houston and California.

Demography has also helped describe the Latino population in the U.S. As of 1989, there were approximately 21 million Latinos constituting under 10 percent of the population of U.S. In the same year, it was projected that there were about 13 million Mexican Americans forming the largest Latino group. There were about 3 million Puerto Ricans while Cuban Americans were about 1 million people in the same year. Other Latino American immigrants were about 4 million people.[54]

The immigration and settlement of Latinos vary from one group to another. It has also varied over time within the groups. During the beginning of the 20th century, Mexican immigrants largely consisted of a rural group that formed migrant worker population. This group joined a settled population predating the 1846 to 1848 wars of Mexican-American by about 250 years. However, from the 1950s, Mexican Americans became more of the urban population mostly concentrated in Texas and California. On the contrary, the initial migration of the Puerto Ricans and Cubans was mostly concentrated in urban areas.

In regard to linguistic affiliations, Spanish forms the national language of the different nations from which Latinos came from and where their culture developed. However, Spanish spoken by American Latinos has changed due to cultural alterations, attitudes, mixtures, and other historical and local incidents as well as syncretism. The Puerto Rican, Mexican, Cuban and other national customs and habits also differ with features of African and American Indian languages. With integration and exposure to American society, many Spanish Speaking Latinos have had their styles and abilities affected by the English language or "Anglicized".

Latinos raised in the United States have even forswore to make use of Spanish to start speaking English. In Latino ethnic identity, language usage has been a key component.

Many Latino populations particularly the recent immigrants and the high social status groups get more pride from their ability to be able to speak fluent Spanish. Some even enjoy their ability of Spanish usage to demonstrate the flair of being bilingual— that is speaking English and Spanish.

At times though, speaking Spanish has resulted in negative personal as well as group experiences. This is because, it has been used by other people or outsiders to stigmatize many of these Latino groups. Even in California, my state of residence and where Latinos outnumber Anglos, I've experienced personally such a stigma.

Mexicans trace their roots to settlement in southwestern U.S. as early as 1598. This is an area, which was colonized by people from Europe before the settlement of New England. This region was one of those areas that were prospering before the arrival of Anglo-Americans in early nineteenth century, something that set in motion events leading to the Mexican-American War dating from 1846 to 1848. The war resulted in culture conflicts and hostility of inter-cultures between the Mexicans and Anglo-Americans.

In the wake of 1910 Mexican Revolution, there was an influx of immigration where the Mexican population mushroomed in all past established settlements. This is a process that has been taking place to this day. The Cubans and Puerto Ricans are associated with U.S. due to the 1898 Spanish-American War.

Spanish is ranked the world's No. 2 language behind Chinese and slightly ahead of English with 329 million speakers. The ranking is determined by the number of people who speak a certain language as their first. Most Hispanics prefer to speak in Spanish even at their homes. However, Spanish is more widely spoken in the U.S. than in Spain.

The United States is the fifth largest Hispanic country in the world registering a high majority consisting of Mexican, followed by Central and South Americans, Puerto Ricans, and Cuban Americans. According to the census done in 2010, Hispanics accounted for more than half of the growth in the U.S.

There are 54 million Latinos and among them are more than 1.1 million Hispanic veterans who served in the United States armed forces. The Latinos who are eligible to vote constitute 25 million, which is approximately the same amount of people living in Texas, which is the second most populated state in the U.S.

The Hispanics are considered to be America's largest ethnic group. Around 60% of people with Hispanic descent have Blood Type O, which is needed the most in hospitals. Caucasians register at 45% while African Americans come in at 50%. Also, Hispanic Cancer Rates show that they are lower as compared to non-Hispanics, marking an even lower rate in lung, prostate, colorectal, and breast cancer.

Today, the Latino community is the second largest ethnic group in the U.S. Those of Mexican origin are the largest group registering two-thirds of the Latinos, which is approximately 34 million, followed by Puerto Ricans with a population of about 4.9 million. Salvadorans, Dominicans, Cubans, Guatemalans and Colombians make up for the rest of the group with more than 1 million people each. About 70% of the Latino community live in Texas, California, New York, Illinois and Florida.

Due to the mixture in cultures in Latin America, foods vary and reflect the Spanish, African, and Asian influences on Latin America as beef, pork, beans, seafood, and various stews are found in all the mentioned groups. Corn products are particularly important in the Mexican and Mexican American culture.

According to Hispanic culture, land and property is transferred to the eldest son, although in some cases elder females are eligible for inheritance as well. However, in present day, most of the traditional practices have been replaced with American practices especially for Latinos and Hispanics who live in the U.S.

Traditionally, when a member of the Hispanic community was ready for marriage the elder family members kept a close watch to make sure there was an appropriate one. Separate Latino groups had their own marriage customs but with time, they learned to incorporate the American cultures. Also, the average age of marriage increased even though it is still lower than the overall average age of marriage in the U.S.

Religion is an important aspect in Latin America. Just as the Spanish language dominates the region, so does Roman Catholicism. Most of Latin American people are Catholics and hold such high belief in the Virgin of Guadalupe. No matter how religious they are, Hispanics highly value the power of fate and destiny.

Sharing is a major aspect when it comes to the Latino and Hispanic culture. They take pride in not only sharing material objects but also information as they are brought up to be cooperative other than competitive. The needs of the family or group holds more ground as compared to the needs of a single individual thus self sacrificing one's needs or beliefs for those of the society is highly prone.

The Hispanic is the closest knit group and takes family very seriously. The family unit extends beyond just nuclear family as they are an all-inclusive group. About 90% of the Hispanic population is Roman Catholic as religion also plays a very important role in their spiritual livelihood and togetherness. Their cooperative nature sees them adapt to certain environments other than control those environments as the uniqueness of an individual is deemed more important compared to individual accomplishment. Hispanics have a tendency of crediting their achievement to fate, religious circumstances or destiny other than their self-ability.

Understanding the Latino Cultures

The first thing you probably notice is that I said "Latino Cultures" in the title and not a single culture. Cramming every Latino into the same box is like saying Americans, Australians, British and South Africans are the same culture because they all speak English. First of all, let's define that we're talking about the Latino culture south of the USA, not the Latino culture of Europe. The American Latino consists of 20 countries.

Mexican Cats Have Seven Lives

Did you know in the USA it's said cats have nine lives? Did you know in Mexico cats have seven lives? No, this will not be on a test, but it's a simple illustration of things you don't know about the culture. To understand it you have to immerse yourself into it. Think about Latino values, family, trajectory, ancestry, dreams for their children, all reflected in every day customs, myths and eventually, political inclinations. Even within a country as vast as the USA, you find different types of music, food, religions and art. This diversity is one of the things that make traveling across the country so interesting. It's the same in large countries that bring immigrants such as Mexico. It is a vast country of more than 120 million with diverse ethnicity, food, music and art. From Mayans to Europeans, you'll find almost every genetic trace that you can imagine.

Two simple things can illustrate the point. Let's place them into context of a movie, a romantic comedy. Any new or old romantic comedy will do as the US values portrayed are well known. A young man lives with his parents and after impossible odds, manages to get a date with his dream girl, who previously dated only the big muscular guy that happens to be a jerk. You know the movie? It's almost every one, right? At a party hosted by his lady, the young man blurts out: "I live with my parents" and everyone laughs at his expense. "What a loser" one of them exclaims placing an L on her forehead using her index and thumb.

This is one of the typical scenes in many movies. You think nothing about it. I look at it and wonder "Why are they making fun of him?" and "Why don't they live with their parents?" They must be really bad people, I might conclude. You see, it's customary for both Latino men and women of any age to live at home until they marry. I married at thirty-one years old and it never even occurred to me to move out of my home. "Who's going to stay with my grandmother?" I thought. When I married, she moved in with my aunt.

This is a very simple example in theory. In practice, it's a very large example of family values and how Latinos might not place as large a weight on independence, placing the entire weight on family. "Why would you want to live your family? Don't you love your family?" If a twenty year old Latino want to move to another state, parents would look for a relative in that state. This way the youngling can stay with them.

Canada, the USA, UK, Australia, New Zealand and other countries share a language and some aspects of culture. However, they are not all the same. They are not all "Anglo's" because they come from the Anglo Saxon culture. They are not all "English" because they share a language or a similar heritage coming from one island. The peoples of Latin-America also share a common language that comes from one country, Spain. However, the mix of race is different, customs, music, food, climate, are all different and especially unique and beautiful.

Blood of my Blood - The Ethnicity inside Latinos

The Americas

Here are some examples of culture from what we know today as Latin-America. Not even close to a complete list, but gives an overview of the diversity of culture and civilization.

Pre-Classic Period (7000- 3000 BC)

Latin America has been home to many indigenous cultures from the earliest life. Archeologist suggest that the first human occupation was at around 7000-8000 BC. Early man followed a seasonal routine that consisted of hunting and gathering around the shores of Lake Titicaca, travelling through the eastern valleys to the desert coast of northern Chile and southern Peru.

Around 6500 BC there was evidence of agricultural practices in Latin America. Foods such as potatoes, chilies and beans started being cultivated in the Amazon Basin. By 3500 BC, Latin American cultures in the highlands of Andes had already started domesticating llamas and alpacas for both transportation and meat. Also guinea pigs were domesticated as a source of food.

By 2000 BC irrigation systems were developed. This gave rise to the Agrarian society as communities had already been settled throughout the Andes and surrounding areas. Fishing along the coast also became a widespread practice that aided in the establishment of fish as the primary source of food. Pottery evidence further suggest that Manioc, which is still a staple food up to date, was being cultivated as early as 2000 BC. The earliest permanent settlers are the Valdivia on the coast of Ecuador. Ceramic works prove their existence from as early as 3500 BC. Other permanent settlers in Latin America during the pre-classic period include:

The Canaris

These were the indigenous natives from Canar and Azuay, today's Ecuadorian provinces. They had elaborate civilization methods, which included advanced architecture and religious beliefs. The Canaris are most known for their fierce resistance against the Incan invasion for many years. Most of their remains were burnt or destroyed from the Incan invasion attacks or later on by the Spaniard attack.

The Chibchas

These occupied part of present day Panama and the high plains of the Eastern *Sierra* Nevada de Santa Marta of Colombia and were composed of several tribes that spoke the same language. Among the tribes were Chitareros, Muiscas, Guanes and Laches. Chibchas were the most in numbers, in socio-economic development and in extended territories of the pre-Hispanic cultures. The areas where the Chibchas occupied were the first ones to develop farms and centuries later these regions were where the independence movement originated and the first industries developed making them the richest areas in Colombia. The Chibchas of eastern and north eastern highlands of Colombia were the most striking people in Latin America.

The Amazonians

These were the Amazon forest dwellers and included tribes such as the Xinguanos. Geological evidence proves that the Amazon was densely populated, however they were affected by diseases from Europe such as small pox. They were divided between dense coastal settlements like Marajo and inland dwellers. Evidence of agricultural practices is seen as the inhabitants of the Amazon managed and developed the soil from the previous hostile environment.

The Classic Period (2600 BC-1000 AD)

The classic period is generally made up of the Andean civilizations. It is a patchwork of different cultures, languages and people that developed from the highlands of Colombia. By the 27th century BC civilization had already started taking place in Latin America. It is proven by existence of the following civilization groups-

Caral Supe

The Caral Supe dates back to the 27th century BC and is among the oldest civilizations in the Americas. It accommodated more than 3000 inhabitants enclosed in an area of more than 60 hectares. It had no signs of warfare as no evidence of weapons or mutilated bodies were found but rather suggested a gentle society that was built on commerce and pleasure. It aided in a rise of urbanism in Mesopotamia. Artifacts discovered were flutes and this suggested a musical background.

Norte Chico

The Norte Chico emerged on the north central coast of Peru during the same time as the Caral civilization. The civilization flourished at the confluence of the Fortaleza, the Pativilica and the Supe Rivers. It completely lacked ceramics and had minimal visual art. The most significant achievement of the Norte Chico was its monumental architecture that included circular plazas and large earthwork platform mounds. Evidence suggests the use of textile technology and the worship of common god symbols. The Norte Chico was founded on seafood and maritime responses.

Chavin

It is a Latin American civilization that established a trade network and developed agriculture in Peru. The Chavin culture began in the Andes highlands and spread throughout the country. It is believed to possibly have originated from a cult, as Chavin de Huantar was an important ritual centre for Chavin.

Nazca

The Nazca culture flourished around 100-800 AD along the dry southern coast of Peru in the river valleys of the Rio Grande de Nazca drainage and the Ica valley. They are known for making beautiful crafts and technologies such as geoglyphs, ceramics and textiles. They built underground aqueducts systems known as puquios that still function to date.

Moche

Alternately known as Mochicha culture, it thrived on the northern part of Peru. They were not politically organized but rather a group of people who shared a common elite culture. The Moche were technologically advanced and traded with faraway people like the Maya. They made ceramic pottery with carvings of their daily lives. They also practiced human sacrificing, blood drinking rituals and their religion incorporated non-procreative sexual practices.

Tiwanaku

They settled in Bolivia around 400 BC near the south eastern shore of Lake Titicaca. The inhabitants of Tiwanaku did not have a written language therefore; most of their culture and history was lost in its demise. However, evidence shows that they made beautiful pottery and textiles. In addition, farming was practiced.

Arawak and Carib

The Arawak lived along the eastern coast of South America, which is present day Brazil up into Guyana. The Caribs are said to have come from Orinoco River and displaced many of the Arawaks. The Caribs were skilled boat builders and sailors who dominated the Caribbean basin with their military skills. They were known for their cannibalism as it made a key part of their war rituals.

Maya

The Maya culture people are thought to have inhabited a vast range of territory including El Salvador, most of southwest Mexico, parts of west Honduras and Guatemala. They used skills they had learnt from other cultures to develop agriculture, which allowed for growth of larger cities.

The early Maya date back to 8,000 to 2000 BC with the early pre-classic period. The Maya evolved and different distinct periods emerged until the Spanish explored their territory first in 1517. Although Maya cities are archeological sites, the people and culture live on in the Yucatan Peninsula.

Inca

The Inca civilization whose capital was the great Puma shaped city of Cuzco dominated by the Andes from 1438-1533. They had no written language but used quipu, a system of knotted strings to record information. They used terrace farming, which was a useful form of agriculture and built their cities with unmatched but precise stonework. There is also evidence of excellent metalwork.

Toltec

They dominated central Mexico between the 11th-13th centuries. They were originally a mixture of tribes dominated by the Nahua speaking Toltec-Chichimecas. Their characteristic feature was guerrilla militarism and professionalism in warfare including mass rituals that involved animal and human sacrifice. They also constructed a rack of skulls as a public display of the heads of their victims.

Aztec

This empire rose in the early 15th century and dominated over the valley of Mexico region. They had a supreme and efficient military force that aided them in extending their territory. They had an adept talent in adopting the artistic styles and skills from their conquered victims. They became the most powerful state in the whole country. The Aztec also performed human sacrifice as a way to glorify their victories in war.

This era was marked by military aggression that saw the demise of most of the empires and civilizations. The post classic era more so reached its peak with the arrival of the Spanish conquest. It is not quite known as per how many indigenous people lived in pre Latin America. However, the number reduced after the Spanish conquest, which also saw the spread of new diseases from Europe.

From Spain to America

Greeks in Spain

According to Greek historian Herodotus, sea captain Kolaios was the first Greek to set foot in Iberia's commonly known Peninsula in the year 640 BC. Kolaios, who was from Aegean island of Samos, was on his way to Egypt when his ship was blown off-course by a storm. He landed in Tartessus where he and his sailors were received by king Arganthonius, also known as man of the silver mountain. Kolaios went back to Samos with a ship full of silver like no other Greek ship had ever returned with.

The Greek commercially expanded along the northeastern part of the Peninsula. The Corinthians established a major colony at Marseille south of France and twenty-five years later another in Emporion on the coast northeast of Gerona. However, Emporion never reached Marseille status but become the principal settlement commercially for the northeast and Greece's major town. Rhodes, a small settlement across the bay from Emporium also played the same role.

The Greeks did not get to penetrate the far inland nor go much beyond the straits of Gibraltar. There is a possibility they were derailed by tales of choking weeds, sea monsters and thick mud brought back by the Phoenicians. The ancient plan of the city of Emporion shows a wall that divided the Greek district from the native section. This confirms that the Greeks did not mingle much with the Iberians who inhabited the Mediterranean Sea as only one gate opened from the wall, which was guarded around the clock.

As evidence of their presence given the years of trade between them and the Iberians, the Greeks left some artifacts such as jewelry, household goods such as ceramics, pottery, pitchers and vases, and other personal items like little clay figures and drinking cups. No one knows what the Iberians called themselves as the name Iberia is owed to them.

Romans in Spain

The Romans arrived in Iberia in 218 BC as a military force with the intent to finish off their rivals, the Carthaginians from whom they had already conquered in other islands. The Carthaginians posed a threat to the Roman expansion as long as they controlled the Peninsula, therefore what resulted was a 12-year war that saw the Carthage power over the Mediterranean.

The Romans claimed to liberate the tribes from the Carthaginian dominance but as soon as they realized the economic potential of the territory, they replaced their previous intentions with permanent residence. Rome divided its newly acquired territory into two provinces namely;

- Hispania Citerior, which included the east coast and inland
- Hispania Ulterior, which is roughly modern Andalusia

At the end the whole area for the first time was controlled by the Romans, with the exception being perhaps the Basque lands.

In conquest to completely rule Peninsula, the Romans encountered enormous resistance from various tribes of the inhabitants of Iberia especially from the Celts of north and North West. The conquest of Hispania is divided into two phases. The first phase involved resistance from the Lusitanians led by a highly vigilant leader and perceived legend Viriatus. He had organizational and military skills that enabled him to cause vast damage as he moved his troops over large areas of the south and south west.

Viriatus was defeated in 138 BC after he was murdered in his sleep by two of his aids that were bribed. Numancia was another barrier when it came to the Roman conquest. Legend has it that after a year long siege, the inhabitants of Numancia chose to set themselves and their city on fire rather than surrender. The second and final phase of the Hispania conquest saw Rome transit from republic and rise to an Empire. It also coincides with the rule of Augustus in 27 BC to 14 AD. After years of conflicts and resistance, the Romans continued persistence finally persevered and peace and prosperity came to the Peninsula. Trade thrived, cities and towns flourished and Hispania completely adapted to the Roman life.

Arabs in Spain

Arabs first came to Spain after crossing the straits of Gibraltar in 711 AD and defeated a Visigothic army conquering Toledo and Cordoba. Within a few years, the Arabs managed to conquer the Christian Visigothic and almost all of the Iberian Peninsula. Hispania was transformed into al-Andalus, which meant Muslim Spain or Islamic Iberia. The Arabs did not impose their religious beliefs on the inhabitants of Hispania but rather allowed the Christians who did not flee to retain their faith and keep their property together with their traditions and laws in related issues such as marriage and divorce, but after signing agreements. The agreements required that Christians pay certain taxes and acknowledge the superiority of Islam.

Most of the Christians of al-Andalus took external trappings of the Muslims in that they adapted to Muslim dress code, eating habits and diets and even learned and spoke Arabic. They were also known as Mozarabs meaning "Arabized". Christians were allowed their own judges and municipal organizations however; disagreements between them and Muslims were settled according to Islamic laws. They were not allowed to repair or construct new churches or synagogues. Converting or attempting to convert Muslims to Christianity was punishable so was dissuading a fellow Christian from converting to Islam.

As a result, Christian males could not marry Muslim women because the women together with their children would then convert to Christianity. Many Mozarabs started using Arab names beside their Hispanic ones especially if their line of work had them working closely with Muslims.

Christians of al-Andalus shared agricultural benefits and better dietary that the other Christians in the north did not. This included fruits such as oranges, watermelons, almonds, bananas, mangoes and lemons. They also had spices such as cinnamon, cumin, nutmeg, cloves, and coriander, and vegetables such as parsnips, carrots, eggplants and spinach.

From the beginning of 1096, the relationship between Muslims and Mozarabs started getting strained. Muslims grew more intolerant and this brought about more repression and discrimination. Many Christians were exiled while others fled to their Christian neighbors. By 1500, Muslim Spain was almost fully demised.

The arrival and settlement of these groups to the Iberian Peninsula in more ways than one brought both benefits and disadvantages especially to the original traditions, cultures and Spanish values. However, certain skills adopted from them helped the Spanish improve in other areas as well. It also influenced the Spanish language as Arabic and Greek words were incorporated. Poetry was also established as a basis of song traditions by the Arabs and was adopted by the Spanish. However, the three groups also benefited and learned new things from the Iberian culture.

A Brief History of American Politics

Growth of populations during those ancient days was marked by the hardships and victories they went through in order to accomplish a certain desired status quo such as financial stability, self-reliance, national unity, economic and technologic development. Change is a necessary evil that most if not all have had to undergo. Sometimes it brews blood baths or economical strains, but the end result most of the time is a solved solution that benefits the future generations. Latin America was no exception to such changes as the events that followed from the preclassic era paved way to the current Latin America.

The history of Latin America has been shaped by certain important events that took place over time, whether in positive or negative aspect but had a significant effect on the population and the making of Latin America's socioeconomic and political structure. Below is a list of some of the historical events that helped shape Latin America into what it is now.

When Christopher Columbus "discovered" the Americas, they had legally belonged to Portugal who had claimed all undiscovered lands on the west. After the return of Columbus both Spain and Portugal allegedly claimed the new lands. This forced Pope Alexander VI to sort out the issue which he issued the bull inter Celera in 1493 that declared Spain owned all new lands west about 300 miles. Portugal was not pleased by the decision made and pressed the matter to a point where the Treaty of Tordesillas was ratified in 1494. This laid down the modern demographics for Latin America as Brazil went to Portugal and Spain got to keep the rest of the New World.

Between 1519-1533, the Spanish established ruthless command in attempt to conquer the Aztec and Inca empires. These two empires had valuable resources that the Spanish desired to possess and therefore they formulated a plan on how to defeat them. The accomplished conquest paved way for enslavement and marginalization of the habitants of Latin America.

The Spanish settled in the New Mexico in 1598 making it the oldest and largest Spanish settlement in the Southwest.

Under the governance of Governor Domingo de Teran, Texas was made a separate Spanish province in 1691.

One of the most prosperous and significant missions was founded in 1718. The San Antonio mission proved to be resourceful as residents could trace down their heritage through the mission's records and oral histories that included traditions handed down from generations to generations. Through archeological investigations, excavations have uncovered traces of original locations of walls, buildings and other architectural artifacts.

In 1776, the Spanish celebrated the founding of San Francisco in the west while the Eastern American colonies were declaring independence from the Great Britain.

During the invasion of Spain by Napoleon, most Latin America countries seized the opportunity by declaring independence from Spain in 1810. In 1825, Mexico, Central and South America attained their independence from Spain. By 1898, the Spanish rule lost their last colonies following the Spanish-American War. With their conquerors out of the way, the new post-colonized American countries were able to rebuild and establish their own identity.

The emergence of the new republican government after Mexico attained her independence from Spain in 1821 ensured that slavery was indefinitely abolished in 1829.

The Mexican-American war took place between 1846-1848. In 1846, Mexico went to war with the United States after continued wrangles on the border. In 1848, the Treaty of Guadalupe Hidalgo was signed and ended the Mexican-American War. The agreement included a territorial settlement, which saw parts of New Mexico, Arizona, Colorado and Wyoming also Nevada, Utah and California cede to the United States.

In late 1864, Uruguay went to war with Brazil and Argentina. Paraguay being an ally of Uruguay decided to offer her military assistance by attacking Brazil. However, Uruguay under a different president joined hands with Brazil and Argentina and fought against her former ally. The war left hundreds of thousands citizens of Paraguay dead and ruins that would take decades to rebuild.

Many Cubans, infuriated by decades of Spanish rule, rose in revolt and many left for the United States and Europe. Following the aforementioned events, the United States adopted the 14th amendment to their constitution and declared all people of Hispanic origin born in the United States to be U.S. citizens in 1868.

In 1870, the Spanish government freed the slaves it owned in Puerto Rico and Cuba. Two years later Puerto Rican representatives won equal civil rights for the colony then a year later, slavery was abolished in Puerto Rico.

Bolivia and Chile went to war in 1879 after spending years quarrelling over a border dispute. Peru an ally of Bolivia decided to offer military assistance and was drawn in to the Chile-Bolivian war. In 1881, the Chilean army captured Lima and started emerging victorious in the bloody battle both on land and at sea. By 1884 Bolivia signed a truce that saw Chile gaining the long disputed coastal province, which left Bolivia landlocked, and also Peru's Arica province.

The United States government handed the government of Cuba to the Cuban people in 1901 after setting certain parameters in place that limited Cuban independence as written in their constitution. The U.S. government enforced that Cuba could not borrow money or sign treaties with other countries unless it was deemed agreeable by them.

However, a year later Cuba declared its independence from the United States.

The Panama Canal was constructed from 1881 and completed in 1914 by the Americans. Completion of the canal saw the change of worldwide shipping and also the secession of Panama from Colombia, which was marked, as a major historical consequence for the people of Panama.

In 1911, the Mexican Revolution took place. It generally involved peasants against the wealthy class and it changed the trajectory of the politics of Mexico as the majority revolted against President Porfirio Diaz. The war brought about gruesome battles, assassinations and massacres but as a result, land reforms finally took place. The war finally came to an end in 1920 after years of conflict. However, in 1921 the United States imposed limitations on the number of immigrants that were allowed in the U.S. for the first time in history. In 1925, border patrol was created.

In 1953 Fidel Castro, his brother and a wagon of ragged followers attacked the Moncada barracks but what they didn't know is that they were establishing one of the most important revolutions known to history. The rebellion grew massively until the Cuban president Fulgencio Batista fled the country in 1959. Castro defied all chances the United States thought of for removing him from power.

John F. Kennedy ran for President in 1960 with Lyndon B. Johnson as his running mate. Johnson sought the expertise of Dr. Hector Garcia to help with the Latino vote. Dr. Garcia formed clubs called Viva Kennedy that massively played a significant role in Kennedy's narrow victory.

On November 22, 1963 President John F. Kennedy was assassinated, leaving his successor as no other than Lyndon B. Johnson. As the new president, Johnson appointed more Mexican Americans to governmental positions than any president before him. He also passed the landmark legislation that advocated for desegregation.

The Civil Rights Acts of 1964 was passed by Congress. The Act established action programs that prohibited discrimination on basis of gender, race, creed, or ethnic background. It also encouraged for equality of employment and opportunities.

In 1968, President Lyndon Johnson started the Hispanic Heritage Week, which later expanded to a month and enacted into law by President Ronald Reagan in 1988. It runs from September 15 to October 15 and celebrates important contributions and influences made by Hispanic and Latino individuals as well as their culture and heritage. September 15th is also the day that El Salvador, Costa Rica, Guatemala, Honduras and Nicaragua commemorate the anniversary of their independence as Mexico, Chile and Belize share their independence in the same month.

From 1980 to 1995, the Hispanic population of Georgia grew by 130% and thus motivated the need to come up with solutions to help the growing population. The Georgia Hispanic Chamber of Commerce was then established first as the Atlanta Hispanic Chamber of Commerce in 1994 whose goal was and still is to represent the interests of Hispanic businesses in the state. There are more than 1300 members now in the organization and has helped more than 59,000 entrepreneurs through the Hispanic American Center for Economic Development that was founded in 2001.

Antonia C. Novello was appointed the first woman and the first Hispanic surgeon general of the United States in 1990 by President George W. Bush.

Between 2004-2010 Arizona had set up strict laws pertaining to illegal immigrants. By 2005, a group of volunteers calling themselves minutemen had began patrolling the border. Their job was to report unauthorized border crossings and any other illegal activities to the U.S. Also in that same year, Antonio Villaraigosa became the first Mexican American mayor.

In April 2010, Arizona Governor Jan Brewer signed the toughest anti-illegal immigrant law in U.S. history. He gave local police unprecedented power to oversee a crack down on anyone employing or sheltering undocumented immigrants. Also in that same year a second generation Cuban American known as Marco Rubio was elected as U.S. senator for Florida.

By 2013, the Latin Americans reached a population of 51 million people making up one-sixth of citizens living in the United States. Over the years, Latin America has undergone changes that absolutely made them a better people with better opportunities after centuries marked with wars and scars of oppression.

The Blood Mix in Spain

Spanish America, due to inter involvement during colonial times instantaneously gave rise to a mixed race population known as Mestizos. Some of the inter-involvement and marriages were forced while others were not. Mestizo in English is translated as mixed and is the Spanish word for the process of mixing ancestries. Traditionally, Mestizo is a term used in Spain and Spanish America to mean a person with combined European and American descent or that born of a European parent and Mestizo parent whether the said person was born in Latin America or elsewhere. The term was used during the time the Spanish empire was in control of their New World colonies to classify their subjects in ethnic or racial categories.

Before the Arabs arrived in Spain we covered some of the different ethnicities and cultures including the Celts, Greek, Roman, and Goths. These cultures came to mix into the Spanish ethnicity and culture. Then, Jews and Moors landed in Spain.

Jews

They are a Jewish ethnic group also known as Sephardic Jews. Sephardim is translated in English as Jewish Spanish or Hispanic. They emerged in the Iberian Peninsula during the beginning of the second millennium and established communities throughout Spain before most were driven away following Alhambra Decree by the Catholic Monarchs. DNA research has proven that 20% of the Iberian Peninsula population has Sephardic Jewish ancestry

Moorish

In AD 711, the Moors, a North African group of people invaded Spain. What followed was years of association between the Moors and the Iberians. However, after unbearable governance from the Umayyad dynasty, Spain and its Muslim Berber dynasty developed religious intolerance. Christians and Jews were forced to convert to Islam and when Christians gained control, they forced Jews and Muslims to convert to Christianity. Studies on genetics revealed that 11% of the Iberian Peninsula also known as Iberia has DNA reflecting the Moorish ancestors.

The Blood Mix in Mexico and Latin America

For many of us mixed race registers to our minds the biracial experience of having one white parent and the other black or Asian. However, for many Latino Americans, mixed race gives them a totally different meaning that is tied to their Latin colonial history. It generally includes having a white and indigenous background somewhere in their ancestry. One third of American Hispanics identify as mixed race.

Mestizo in Spanish means mixed and is used throughout Latin America to describe a person of mixed race where as Mulatto in Spanish refers to a mixed race that includes white European and black African roots. Mestizo makes up a larger majority in Mexico and the Andean countries of South America while the Mulatto makes up smaller shares in the aforementioned countries. However, in Brazil where population with African ancestry is large there are more Mulattos.

Mixed race in Latin America has helped produce a rich culture through its many influences that brought about the said mixed race, and they include:

Pre Colombia

Before the conquest and colonization, people from different parts of Latin America had already inter-married and this brought about one of the earliest mixed races. Ethnic groups before the conquest socially mingled, traded together and this resulted in a lot of inter involvement. The classic period were war and guerilla attacks existed between power hungry empires also significantly aided blood mix especially in Mexico, Paraguay, Ecuador, Bolivia, and Peru.

European

During colonization of Latin America by European countries, Spain, France, and Portugal marked the beginning of a new culture. This imperial culture not only left a permanent mark by influencing the language which is now used by most Latin American countries and some parts of the United States but also brought about the original idea of the Mestizo, which as mentioned meant a person with European and Latin American heritage. It brought about a significant percent of mix blood throughout Latin America.

Africa

The African culture to Latin America was brought about by the Africans who survived the Trans Atlantic slave trade. It had influences in music, dance, religion and cuisine in Latin American countries such as Brazil, Panama, Dominican Republic, Haiti, Cuba, Colombia and Puerto

Rico. This also resulted in blood mix between the Africans and the habitants of the mentioned countries.

Others

They include the Filipino, Chinese, Japanese, and Indian immigrants and laborers who arrived from the coolie trade. They influenced the culture of Cuba, Peru, Panama, and Brazil in areas such as art, food, and cultural trade and in the end, blood mix was inevitable.

In the 19th and 20th century, a lot of immigration took place, which enhanced blood mix to and from those regions such as Germany, Italy and Eastern Europe. Today blood mix goes beyond global borders as times have changed and co-relating with people from other countries and continents has become easier. Traveling and relocating either for work or personal purposes has greatly aided in blood mix and interrelations between Hispanics and the rest of the world. This also helps in spreading and teaching their culture to others in however small ways it can considering the effects of the Western and American culture in today's world.

Conservative Values, Democratic Voters

Latinos cling to conservatives' views in a number of important issues, but Latinos give their votes to Democrats before the political candidates and campaign managers are effective at mobilizing and influencing them to vote in favor of the liberals as, John Mendez who is Director of Faith Initiatives for The LIBRE Initiative said in an interview with *The Christian Post*. A major question that has been lingering in minds of many Americans and particularly the Republicans is; why do Latinos vote for the Democrats if they are conservatives? According to Mendez, the first reason is that Democrats have made efforts to reach Hispanics and pass across their message. They have put a lot of effort in to reach Hispanics— they go where they are at, they also educate them, they engage them in conversation, and recruit them. The record reason according to Mendez[55] is that Republicans have not made much effort to reach Latinos. Latinos are influenced by a conservative message and when they hear it, they discover that they are not liberal, they happen to be conservatives.

Most Hispanics in the U.S. are associated with the Catholic Church, but nowadays, their share in that religious community or group is diminishing.

Miguel Contreras, in his conversation with the gentleman he met at the open house event, had further discussions not only touching on political but also social and religious aspects. In the conversation, the Gentleman wanted to dig more from Miguel and now that he was getting uncomfortable, he switched the conversation to a different topic. They both found themselves talking about religion. Previously in the conversation, they had touched on immigration and the Syrian crisis. The gentleman had raised an issue about why we shouldn't accept refugees. He had mentioned why German and Europe shouldn't accept refugees. In the same breath he had quickly said "I am a Christian; don't get me wrong, I am not a racist." And Miguel being a Christian, he said, "As Christians, we are called to help those in need."

Miguel wanted to see the reaction of the gentleman. The gentleman reacted with a blank stare in the face meaning probably Miguel's words had pinned him down now that he said he's Christian. Maybe to say, should Christians not help people like refugees who are in need? Again, this presented a different view about Miguel's perception and points of view on Christianity and the beliefs.

The conversation changed from one thing to another and landed inevitable on immigration. Miguel pointed out that "Americans" were so lucky to live in a country where they are comfortable.

"It's so unfortunate people have to leave our country and migrate to another, many times without even knowing about the culture". Miguel himself never went through what immigrants go through but his parents did.

Miguel's thoughts on immigrations are eye-opening. "Imagine things are so bad, so unbearable in your home, the place you love, that you have to leave." He says. "Those people couldn't even think of coming to the U.S. if they knew they would not get opportunities."

The conversation with Miguel's new acquaintance continued. "They are breaking the law, they are doing something illegal" said the elderly gentlemen. "These people are coming to seek for jobs. Is seeking for jobs breaking the law?" he asked. "These are people who are going to be absorbed in manual jobs like construction workers, gardeners, and such. They are helping grow the economy." Miguel concluded.

The conversation continued. "Some immigrants even work in white-collar jobs, but because they're separated by color, race or accent they are not allowed." Miguel continued. As a businessman, Miguel argued that because of labor law abuse where immigrants are paid below the standard wage levels, the cost of some products is actually down. For example, given the economic situation in the U.S. Americans are not prepared to pay $50 for a hamburger. Americans now can get a burger at about $3 or so dollars because the cost of production is low. This is because the so labeled illegal immigrants are providing cheap labor. But technically, these are not illegal immigrants.

On explaining how the people labeled as illegal immigrants are helping businesses to cut down on cost, the gentleman began to see the logic in it. In fact, the conversation shifted and they were now resonating and reasoning at par. The gentleman could see the economic sense of the illegal immigrants and also being a businessman himself, he started supporting Miguel's views. The gentleman runs a small construction company and actually employed the cheap labor that he argues to deport.

Miguel Contreras mentioned that it is that cheap labor that gave him (the gentleman) an edge to cut down on cost. In many ways, the construction company of that gentleman was making more money because it could cut down on cost of labor. After brilliantly being explained this point, guess what? The gentleman said, "You know what Miguel, I think we should bring the Bracero program back!"

The republican gentleman was thinking and could see beyond the logic. The Bracero is a program intended to bring guest permitted workers to the U.S.

The topic changed to the other difficult one, religion.

The gentleman asked Miguel, "…and, what is your religion?" Miguel replied, "I am a fellow Christian!" The gentleman said, "… yeah, you are Christian but what denomination?" Miguel knew where the gentleman was heading in this conversation. He assumed that if Miguel was Mexican, he must be Catholic. Jokingly, Miguel told the gentleman that he is a non-Catholic Christian. In Latino culture, non-Catholic Christians is a growing trend according to Miguel. "Yes," Miguel repeated, "I'm not Catholic,"

Miguel Contreras has a small team in real estate sales. He does business in the real estate industry. He has a network that consists of all races, colors and religions. He doesn't see his network in the real estate industry as Latinos. A lot of Latinos have a perception about themselves that they can only network with other Latinos. This is however a disadvantage to them. However, Contreras sees that anyone is of great value to him in his personal life or business. Whether you are white, black, blue, or whichever color, Contreras networks with anybody.

Most Latinos vote Democrats but are conservatives. They have conservative values in things like money, family, religion and other aspects of life. Latinos feel that if a party is against them, it can't get their vote.

There is so much hate speech pointing to immigrants like Latinos. Miguel Contreras is a Republican because of partly his entrepreneurial role. He doesn't agree with bigger government. He is pro-gay marriage and feels that the social values brought up by Republican candidates resonates with him. He is one of a growing young entrepreneurial republicans. Educated, respectful of other's religion and values, pro-immigration, and at the same time in favor of a small government and lower taxes.

Contreras felt that if he was a Democrat, he couldn't even have entered into conversation with the elderly republican gentleman. This is because the gentleman could have felt that this is one of us therefore, that situation could open up a conversation.

If you are in the business of politics, you're in the business of votes. The votes are your revenues in the sphere of marketing. When a candidate says Latinos or immigrants are bad people, it means that he or she doesn't want the vote. He or she is turning down the "revenue" which in this case is the vote.

Some politicians try to draw straight lines. I'm pro-Latino but anti-immigration. Or I'm for legal immigration. Without knowing any specifics about Latinos and immigration this may sound logical. After all, we're all for obeying the law. In truth this is not a clear line in the sand matter. Legal immigration could mean immigration of the rich. Supporting Latinos and not immigration reform is an oxymoron. Most Latinos are immigrants, and many have family or friends considered undocumented at some point in their lives.

Why do Latinos vote democrat if they're conservatives?

"Latinos are Republicans. They just don't know it yet" - Ronald Reagan.

Ronald Reagan once famously quipped that "Latinos are Republicans. They just don't know it yet." The Republican Party's overriding priority in the years ahead must be to expand and diversify its shrinking demographic base, embracing immigrants generally and Hispanics in particular.
Source: Immigration Wars, by Jeb Bush, p.206, Mar 5, 2013

Most Latinos are religious (55 percent say they are Catholic, 22 percent say they are evangelical Protestants with only 18 percent being unaffiliated,[56] according to a 2013 National Survey of Latinos and Religion by the Pew Research Center). Most Latinos also have extended families and hold nothing more dearly than their family. Not family as we see it in the USA, but extended family. This means cousins, uncles, aunts, grandfathers, godfathers, even second or third cousins are an integral part of your family and could even live in the same house. Latinos are fiscal conservatives in the view of money both in politics and in their own household. They're attracted to right wing religious values but not at the extreme, most of them being of Catholic origin. All the republican buzz words are part of everyday life for Latinos living in the USA as well as their extended family living in other countries. If they act like conservatives, think like conservatives, and talk like conservatives, why do they vote Democrat most of the time?

More often than not Latinos have been characterized to be more conservative in regards to the social aspect. However, when it comes to their own assessment of their political views, Latinos often say that their views are liberal contrary to what the general public might perceive them as.

According to the July 2013 U.S. Census Bureau, population was estimated at roughly 54 million Hispanics living in the United States representing approximately 17 percent of the entire U.S. population making the people of Hispanic origin the largest ethnic minority group in the U.S. Solely Mexican Americans represent 64 percent of Hispanics and they tend to lean more on the Democrats side, therefore the Democratic Party is considered to be in a far stronger position among the Hispanics in general. The U.S. census indicates that the Hispanic population in the United States is the fastest growing minority group in the country.

The reason why most Mexican Americans prefer the Democrat party dates back to the different experiences they have had while migrating to the U.S. as compared to Cubans, who are traditionally Republicans. When Cubans are caught on the border without documentation they're granted refuge if they at least have one foot on U.S. soil. During the Fidel Castro regime, which lasted until 2008 before replaced by his brother Raul Castro, banks in the U.S. gave small business loans to Cuban exiles who had no credit or collateral in the country. With such startup capital, the immigrants from Cuba were best placed by the American establishment to thrive financially. Their neighborhoods and communities were able to develop robust economic and political systems to support the success of new incoming Cuban immigrants thus giving their descendants a first class lane to join the American elite.

Immigration policy is just the start of the Cuban immigrant's advantage. Cuban immigration is among the least in terms of Latin American immigrants registering at 1 percent of the U.S. population, however, they are uniquely placed to receive such power and status that in just one generation can produce a candidate or two ready to enter the political scene on a national level.

However much, it is not surprising that the two Hispanic frontrunners in the presidential race of 2016, Marco Rubio and Ted Cruz are both Republicans. Compared with the rest of the Hispanic population in the U.S., as a result of the advantageous treatment of Cuban immigrants, they have a higher level of education, higher rate of home ownership and higher median household income.[57]

On the other hand, Mexican Americans inherited a legacy of discrimination that dates back to the founding of the United States during the controversial Mexican-American War that resulted from a border dispute that had been ongoing. Mexico eventually ceded Texas, California and the land in between, to the United States and acknowledged by historians to be a land grab of dubious moral imperative.

After continued legal fights over the stolen lands aside from those that were ceded, the Americans started a tradition of red-lining Mexican American citizens up to the 1980s. The end result was economically depressed neighborhoods and even the entire region which is still felt up to date. This has also led to other immigrants throughout Latin America to be incorporated in the poorest communities in the U.S. leaving the Hispanic Americans with depressingly low rates of educational attainment and high poverty, unemployment, poor health and incarceration rates.

Such circumstances hardly provide a pool full of high level politician talent thus the reasons why Mexican Americans and other Hispanics still do not appear in positions of national political power in proportion to their large numbers considering that there are only two Latino governors and both are Republicans.

Based on a 2010 report from a survey done by the Pew Hispanic Center, it highlighted that Hispanics rank education, health care, and jobs as their top three issues with immigration coming in as the fourth most important issue for all Latinos. Most Mexican Americans believe that these four main issues that are important to them have, in one way or another, tried to be met. The steps taken include increasing of income, ensuring paid family leave, making debt free college a reality, improving on healthcare and fixing the broken immigration systems. These issues are, however, best represented by the list of Democratic Presidential candidates thus the reason they still vote Democrat whilst they are naturally conservatives.

The following are among a few more reasons why Latinos vote for Democrats despite their conservative attributes:

The main dividing wall between Hispanics and Republicans is the fact that both of them differ in certain views especially on perceived cruel public speaking on illegal immigration and racism, as 81 percent of Latino population feel that undocumented immigrants need not be deported whereas some Republicans support the idea of deportation. Other Republicans also advocate for efforts to enforce the law, which is deporting all illegal aliens while some Republicans are open to welcoming the idea of accepting back immigrants who enter America through legal avenues.

Generally, the Republican Party has been doing an exceptionally shoddy job in recruiting Latin Americans into their party aside from South Floridian Cubans. As the demographics in California, New York, Illinois, and Texas are changing, an aspect that would seem like the most opportune moment for the Republican Party to secure new political strongholds by recruiting Latinos, the Republican Party still remains adamant to do so, hence the party has suffered immensely.

From the moment the Republican Party realized that the demographics were working against them, it would have seemed a sound and logical idea to support some of the forums that the Latinos were requesting such as bilingual education and some of the support programs for potential voters. Instead, they strongly and openly opposed them.

During years of war between the U.S. and some of Latin America countries, both former Republican Presidents Ronald Reagan and Bush were involved. These two presidents fought wars between the years of the 1980s and 1990s from the Contras to Guatemala and Panama. The result of the war saw to it that tens of thousands of Latinos lost their lives sponsored by the U.S. Most people presume that because it happened a long time ago, the bad memories are not still engraved in minds and hearts of most Latinos leaving in the U.S. as a result of being refugees, a product of the war.

Puerto Rico is an island that has more potential votes than any other does. This is a territory that has more people than 16 states combined and instead of the Republican Party to work on strategies to acquire these votes it ceded the Island to the Democrats. The Republican Party has come down really hard over the statehood of Puerto Ricans for many years instead of pressing for the statehood and recruiting more voters.

The number of Latino voters have leaned towards democrats because of the Democratic Party´s platform for less restrictions on immigration issues, civil rights, and support for social programs that benefit low-income Latino families. Over the years, some Latino leaders have ridiculed the party for not doing as much as they would to help Latino candidates to move from city council, legislative, and congressional seats to the party´s highest elected offices.

More than nine percent of eligible voters in the nation are Latino and the majority support leaning towards Democratic candidates continues the prototype among Hispanic voters. In poll rates conducted sometimes in December 2011, close to 67 percent of Hispanic indicated they were Democrats, while 20 percent said they were Republicans.

In 2010-midterm elections, 60 percent of Hispanics voted Democrats while 38 percent voted Republicans. In 2008, 6 percent of Latin Americans voted for presidential candidate Barack Obama, while 31 percent of them voted for presidential Republican candidate John McCain.

In 2006, the number of Latino voters who supported Democratic candidates in congressional races was 69 percent, while 30 percent supported Republican candidates.

We talked about how President Ronald Reagan once famously said that most Latinos were Republicans but they just didn't know it. This quote is often used by the Republican Party and relies on the notion that most Latinos are conservative in regards to social issues such as reproductive rights, marriage equality, abortion and homosexuality

Religion plays a very huge role in the politics of a country and in this case the church because the U.S. is dominated by Christians. Latinos are a group of religious observant and compared to the general public, they are the most likely to claim a religious affiliation and attend a religious service more frequently. They are also most likely to say religion is important to their lives.

Overall, religion significance is higher among immigrant Latinos and lowest among third generation Latinos. A Pew Hispanic survey states that 83 percent of Hispanics claim to be religiously affiliated just slightly higher than the general public at 80 percent. [58]

According to a survey done by Pew Research more than 68 percent of Hispanics identified themselves as Catholics, 19 percent as protestants while 14 percent claim no affiliation to any religion.[59]

In the survey, among Hispanics, 13 percent were more likely to say they are Protestants while only 6 percent identified with other religions such as Mormonism, Orthodox Christianity and Judaism or Buddhism. Therefore, compared to the general public, Hispanics are more likely to be Catholic at 62 percent versus 23 percent, and less likely to be protestant with 19 percent versus 50 percent while the general public is more likely to be unaffiliated to any religion at 19 percent compared to the Hispanics at 14 percent.[60]

Overall, 61 percent of Latinos said that religion is very important to them and 24 percent said that religion is somewhat important while 13 percent say religion is not too important.[61]

However, there is a shifting dimension in regard to religious affiliation among Hispanics. The number of Catholic Hispanics is reducing as more join the protestants wing, as evident in the 2013 National Survey of Latinos and Religion conducted by the Pew Research Center.

When the religious aspect of Latin Americans run concurrently with political ideology, there is often a split between liberal and conservative prospects. Latino Catholics as well as Latino Protestants are in an even way split among the three groups. Among the population of religiously unaffiliated Latinos, almost twice as many claim that their political views are liberal or very liberal at 45 percent, more than those who say that their political views are conservative or very conservative at 23 percent.[62]

Comparing them with the general public, Latino population is somehow more liberal and this disparity is greater within Latino Evangelical Protestants who are three times more likely to call themselves liberal or very liberal with 25 percent more than the general public at 8 percent.

On issues such as abortion, gay marriage or homosexuality, religious influence in politics, and divorce most Latinos tend to think conservatively. This tends to create tension for the traditional political categories in the U.S. simply because when addressing issues such as immigration, government guaranteed health insurance or a willingness to pay higher taxes for better government services, most of the Latinos often lean on the side that is considered liberal.

For example, the tension between Latino Pentecostals and evangelicals was apparent in 2008 when both voted for President Barack Obama, and for proposition 8— the

Californian measure that defined marriage as a union between a man and a woman.

The Catholic Church's stance on homosexuality is based on a distinction between being lesbian or gay and acting on it; they accept the former and consider the latter as wrong and sinful. This results in condemnation of LGBT Latinos in communities of faith and has led most of them to remain closeted where religious activities are involved.

When Latinos are asked whether homosexuality ought to be accepted or discouraged in the society, about 59 percent of them and about 58 percent of the U.S. general public say it should be accepted while 30 percent of Latinos and 33 percent of the general public say that homosexuality should be discouraged. However, views on homosexuality seem to vary by immigrant generation. About 53 percent of Hispanic immigrants say homosexuality should be accepted while 68 percent of second generation Hispanics say it should be accepted and 63 percent among third generation Hispanics think the same.[63]

In the case of attitudes about abortion, a great majority of Hispanic Catholics and Protestants believe that abortion should be illegal in all if not most cases. Latino Protestants are somehow likely to have a higher percentage in regards to abortion at 65 percent than Latino Catholics who are at 52 percent. Similarly, Hispanics who are religiously unaffiliated say abortion should be illegal with 32 percent but the great majority accounting 62 percent are of the idea that it should be legal.

Support for abortion rights vary by age, not by gender. Young generation Latinos are for the idea that abortion should be legal, while the older ones say it should be illegal in all cases.

Latino families are a very close knit entity and tend to be highly group-oriented. A strong emphasis is often placed on the Latino family because it is the source from where an individual gets their identity and protection when times are hard. However, this intense sense of belonging and togetherness is limited to family and close friends. People who are neither friends nor family might take time being trusted.

The family model is an extended one with grandparents, aunts, uncles, cousins, and other closely related people being considered as part of the immediate family. This supreme joint loyalty given to extended family is also known as 'familismo'. Any member of the familismo is expected to financially support the family and vice versa, as it is considered very important.

In the familismo setup, there isn't room for individuality as the decision and behaviors of an individual are solely based on pleasing the family. Decisions cannot be made by the individual member without consulting with the family first.

More often than not, conflicts, non compliance and dissatisfaction of services especially healthcare come about when, for example, if a health practitioner is unaware of the familismo dynamics, the family can holdup important medical decisions because the extended family members' consultation may be very time consuming.

In order to gain the confidence and trust of a Latino patient, it is significantly important for the practitioner to solicit opinions from other members of the family who may be present and give ample time for the extended family to consult on the matter at hand.

From generations of Hispanics present during the World Wars, there came a need to raise young men with machismo attitudes so that they can be soldiers to fight the war. This promoted heteronomy as only strong and virile men are considered to be real men up to date.

Even though divorce is on the rise in most Latin American cultures, it is viewed as sin and carries with it great social and moral stigmas. In fact, most Hispanic literature speaks of divorce as a sin that should be avoided. Marriage is emphasized as a holy and eternal union that should not be broken. Socially, divorce often results in isolation and alienation by both families against the spouse perceived as causing the divorce. As a result of this, many couples simply separate and start new families.

Work is an important aspect of livelihood to Latinos because it is their duty to financially cater for the familismo whether in the U.S. or back at home. Immigration has always been caused by the need for better jobs and opportunities to give the Latino families a better life.

Undocumented workers or illegal aliens cross the border to come work in factories, construction sites, in homes and hotels, and poultry farming so that they are able to sustain the families they have. The USA has more job opportunities and better paying jobs than Mexico and other Latin countries, and that's why so many Latinos immigrate consistently.

When it comes to money, Latinos tend to say they are conservatives because they are pro lower taxes, smaller governments and less government regulation of business, thus they claim to be fiscally conservative on economic issues but socially liberal. This often brings confusion as to where Latinos stand. One cannot separate fiscal issues from social values as they are deeply intertwined and affect each other.

More often than not, economic issues tend to be social issues and vice versa. Conservative fiscal policies do enormous social harm even the most generous of the policies. It is such policies that pave the way for perpetuation of Human Rights abuses. The policies make life a misery for people who may be said to be encountering hard lives, already. Regardless of how pure intended the people supporting those policies are, the policies are racist, sexist, classist, homophobic, transphobic and in other words socially retrograde.

In so many ways, they do more harm than social policies that are allegedly separate from economic ones. The aforementioned issues make it difficult to know where the Latino loyalty in regard to votes comes in as they can change their minds based on the party that well represents their issues.

The former governor of Florida, Jeb Bush who had relationships with the state's large Hispanic population said that If you accept as true the conservative philosophy as he does, then it would be very stupid over the long term to pay no attention to the rapidly increasing Hispanic votes. Jeb further said that the point of view of Hispanics holds to conservative ideologies and political candidates are seemingly becoming brighter than before.

However, when it comes to political ideologies, Latinos are evenly distributed across the conservatism and liberal spectra. Latino Catholics and Latino Protestants are evenly split some leaning on the conservative side while the other on the liberal one.

Due to the Hispanic strong commitment to religion and family, the Republicans have a greater chance of pursuing the Latino Vote if they can change their party's philosophy and deal with the four immediate issues that are listed by most Latinos including increased employment capacities, better health care plans, affordable college and better immigration policies to fix the current broken system.

Immigration policies regardless of being the fourth on the list of most pressing issues, it is something that needs to be rationalized giving a balance between deportation and amnesty. As evident as it has been seen, the shared values between Republicans and the conservatism nature of Latinos is one aspect that should not be taken lightly or for granted because they may share the same ideologies on policies but one wrong move or word will send Latinos voting for Democrats until the Republicans can work on ways to meet them halfway.

On the other hand, as Democrats keep fulfilling the needs of Latinos including the Obamacare, by offering better health services and striving to increase Job opportunities, they will continue to get Latino votes despite them being conservative-oriented.

Conservatism is good for Hispanics in that they call for less dependency on state welfare and gives rise to better livelihood. It is through conservatism that issues on lack of employment and poor health services can be tackled and adversely dealt with. It is the best way to deal with increasing issues of poverty. The puzzle on how Republicans are going to influence the Latinos to vote for them squarely lies on how they understand, identify, and resolve issues surrounding their family, culture, social needs, economic needs, religion, and political motives.

History of Immigration

In the late 15th and early 16th century Latin America was home to many indigenous people many of whom had advanced civilizations including the Aztec, Inca, Muisca and the Maya. However, in the early 19th century a majority of the region had attained its independence thereby forming its new countries with some remaining colonies.

During the colonial era most of the immigration comprised of the Spanish and Portuguese settlers as well as some overseers from France and Netherlands. Also, a huge number of black African slaves were brought in where they were sold to the sugar plantations in the West Indies or the plantations in Brazil. A large scale immigrant movement occurred between 1840s and 1914 mostly to Cuba, Argentina, Brazil, Venezuela, Chile and Uruguay. Most of these new immigrants came from Italy, Britain, Spain, Germany and some from Japan and China as well.

In 1845 Texas was officially annexed to the United States. This angered the Mexican government as conflict over the border line began. Around April 1846, Mexico and the United States went into war over the disputed territory. On June 14th 1846, Mariano Guadalupe Vallejo, a Military Commander of California was woken up by a fuming mob consisting of Anglo-settlers who forced him to put his sign on the Articles of Capitulation to make California an independent republic.[64]

Between 1848 and 1853 Mexico surrendered and what followed was the selling of the land between Arizona, Mesilla Valley, Yuma, and New Mexico by the then returning President of Mexico called Antonio Lopez Santa Anna, to the United States.[65]

In 1859 Cigar factories were constructed in Florida, Louisiana, and New York bringing a massive migration of working class Cuban immigrants to the growing industry in the United States. By 1862, the Homestead Act was passed in Congress that allowed squatters in the West to settle and claim unoccupied lands, many of, which were owned by Mexicans.[66]

In 1868, Cubans rose in revolt angered by 300 years of Spanish rule. This prompted many to migrate to Europe and the United States and as a result, the U.S. adopted the 14th amendment to its constitution, which declared all people of Hispanic origin born in the United States to be Citizens of the U.S. This move prompted the Spanish government to free the slaves it owned in Cuba and Puerto Rico in 1870.

On April 6th 1917, the United States declared that it would confront and fight Germany thereby joining the First World War. With many physically fit men off to the fight in the war, impermanent Mexican workers were allowed and

157

given permission to enter and work in the United States. By May of the same Year, the Selective Service Act became law obligating Mexican immigrants in the United States to register for the draft despite them being not eligible.

By 1921, a limited number of immigrants was allowed in the United States as imposed for the first time in the history of the United States. In 1925, the Border Patrol was created by Congress and by 1932, the U.S. government began to deport Mexican immigrants. Around 300,000 and 500,000 Mexican Americans were forcefully driven out of the United States.[67]

In the 1940s, during the time when the Second World War took place, many Latinos enlisted in the U.S. military making them the largest ethnic group serving in the war. Following this move, the Fair Practices Act was passed that encouraged equal employment rights and discouraged discrimination in employment. Due to the labor shortage caused by the Second World War, the U.S. government launched an agreement with Mexico to import temporary workers to fill the work spaces left in the agricultural field.

In 1944, a program known as Operation Bootstrap was initiated by Puerto Rico to encourage industrialization and also to meet the U.S. labor demand. This ignited a massive wave of migrant workers to the United States. This relationship also helped Puerto Rico to gain political autonomy in 1947, as it became a member of the common wealth.

The Bracero program was officially launched in 1951. It was part of the Mexican Farm Labor Supply program. In the Mexican labor agreement, it concluded that an approximately 350,000 Mexican workers were to be brought in to the United States until the end of the program in 1964. During this period, the Supreme Court recognized that Latinos were suffering from inequality and discrimination, which paved the way for Hispanic Americans to use legal means to fight.

Between 1954 and 1958, Operation Wetback was put into place by the United States government. Its initiative was the government's effort to seek, find, and send home or deport undocumented workers. During the four-year period 3.8 million people of Mexican descent were deported.[68]

In 1962, the community service organization turned down Cesar Chavez's request as their president to organize farm workers. As a result, Cesar and Dolores Huerta resigned from the organization and later went to form the National Farm Workers Association. In 1964, Congress passed the Civil Rights Act. It established affirmative action programs that prohibited discrimination on basis of gender, race or ethnic background. It proposed equality of employment opportunities and removed barriers that operated in the past. This was to prevent job discrimination. The Bracero program that was initially put in place during World War II came to an end.

In 1966, workers who had gone on strike were subjected to not only physical but also verbal attacks as they engaged in their peaceful demonstrations. On March 16th in Delano, the Senate Sub-Committee on migratory labor held their hearings. The following day, Cesar Chavez set out with a hundred of his workers to begin his pilgrimage to San Joaquin Valley. Twenty-five days later, their numbers went from hundreds to an army of thousands, which prompted the state capital to meet with union representatives.

In the spring of 1980, Fidel Castro announced that any Cuban who wished to leave Cuba may do so. Following a period of five months, more than 125,000 Cubans arrived in South Florida. The newly arrived Cubans were branded as either mentally ill or criminal even though only four percent were from mental hospitals, about 25,000 were implicated with criminal records.[69]

President Ronald Reagan signed the Immigration Reform and Control Act in attempt to control illegal immigration and maintain a stable agricultural labor force. The act was intended to toughen the United States immigration law and border security. This enforced that employers monitor the immigration status of the employee. The Act also granted amnesty to close to three million immigrants consisting mostly of Mexicans who had sneaked through the border unnoticed from the 1970s to the 1980s.

On November 8th 1994, Californians passed Preposition 187 with 59 percent of the vote. This resulted in the ban of undocumented immigrants from receiving public education and benefits such as subsidized healthcare and welfare. This made it a felony offense to produce, supply, sell or try to use falsified residence or citizenship documentations. It also required any city, county or state officials to report any suspected or alleged illegal aliens. In 1996, the preposition 187 was ruled unconstitutional on the grounds that only the federal government had the authority to regulate immigration.

In 2004, anti-immigrant sentiments reached a breaking point when the residents of Arizona decided to organize a group of volunteers known as The Minutemen to patrol the border. By April 2005, the Minutemen had begun patrolling the border and reporting unauthorized border crossings and other illegal activities to the U.S. border patrol. With no new comprehensive federal immigration policies in place, different states began to implement their own. In April, Arizona's governor Jan Brewer signed the harshest and toughest anti-illegal immigration law in the history of the United States. The legislation suggested crack downs on anyone hiring or harboring undocumented immigrants. The law also gave local police unprecedented authority.[70]

Georgia, following Arizona's legislation made sure that anyone who was stopped for not having a driver's license or unable to provide proof of residency could be forwarded to the immigration authorities. Immigration of the of the Hispanic and Latino population from Latin America has had a massive impact on the population of the United States since time immemorial. History has seen the expansion of Latin and Hispanic population from 3.24 percent in the 60's to an astounding 16 percent of the nation's population in present time in the U.S. Of the 16 percent, more than a third resided in other South American countries while the rest of the population was spread throughout Europe and North America.

The United States is the leading destination for Latin American immigrants with 25 percent, followed by Spain at 16 percent then Argentina at 15 percent and Venezuela at 10 percent. By 2014, the largest Latin American countries of origin with immigrants were Colombia at 25 percent followed by Peru at 16 percent, Ecuador at 15 percent, Brazil at 12 percent and Guyana at 10 percent and together they accounted for 77 percent of the total South American immigrant population.

Immigration from Latin America rapidly grew between 1960 to 1980 and they continue to impact the social, economic, and political life in the United States. More than 56 percent of Latin American immigrants have settled in three states with Florida having the most with 24 percent followed by New York with 21 percent and New Jersey 11 percent. The leading four counties having the most immigrants as of 2010-2014 were Florida's Miami-Dade County, Queens County in New York, Florida's Broward County, and Los Angeles County in California. These counties accounted for about 26 percent of the immigration population in the U.S.

Latin American immigrants were more likely to be proficient in English as compared to the overall foreign-born population. About 45 percent of Latin American immigrants aged 5 and above reported limited proficiency in the language as compared to 50 percent of all immigrants. Close to 2 percent of immigrants from Guyana were limited in English proficiency while Argentina had 35 percent, Venezuela had 38 percent, Chile had 39 percent, Brazil and Bolivia registered a 40 percent each of individuals with limited English proficiency. Meanwhile, 52 percent of Peruvians, 53 percent of Colombians, and 65 percent of Ecuadorans reported limited English proficiency.

The median age for Latin America immigrants was 45 years as compared to the foreign-born who had a median of 44 years and 36 years for those born in the U.S. By 2014, Latin American immigrants who were working were aged between 18 to 64 and less likely to be under the age of 18 as compared to the native and foreign-born population. Most Latin American immigrants were of the working age with Brazil accounting for 89 percent, Venezuela at 85 percent, and Ecuador at 83 percent. Those aged 65 and older that were working was Chile with 20 percent, Brazil with 18 percent and Guyana with 17 percent.

Annexation of Mexico Territory to the United States

Annexation is the political transition of land from the control of one entity to another and in this case involving Mexico and the United States. Following decades of wrangles involving the border dispute, war finally broke out and marked the beginning of the famous Mexican-American War. It was brought about by whether Texas, which had been annexed by the U.S., ended at Nueces River claimed by Mexico or at Rio Grande claimed by the U.S.

A treaty known as Guadalupe Hidalgo, negotiated by Nicholas Trist, who was the chief clerk of the State Department. The treaty which was signed in 1848, brought an end to the war; it also suggested that Rio Grande was the border between the two countries in conflict ceding a large chunk of land to the U.S. Mexico agreed to sell its territory North of the Rio Grande for a sum of $15 million and an agreed amount of $3.25 million in debts that Mexico owned to the U.S. citizens.[71]

Some of the land sold to them are among present day California, Utah, Nevada, Arizona, New Mexico and Wyoming. Over 90 percent of the Mexicans occupying the mentioned lands chose to become U.S. citizens. The land that the treaty Guadalupe Hidalgo ceded to the U.S. became part of the U.S. between 1950 and 1912: California in 1850, Nevada in 1864, Utah in 1896 and Arizona in 1912.

Depending upon interpretation, the entire state of Texas was purchased in 1845, which then included part of Kansas in 1861, Colorado in 1876, Wyoming in 1890, Oklahoma in 1907 and New Mexico in 1912. The remaining bit of the Southern parts of New Mexico and Arizona were peacefully purchased through the treaty of Mesilla under the Gadsden Purchase, which saw the U.S. an additional of $10 million. This land was meant to accommodate the transcontinental railroad.[72]

The treaty extended U.S. citizenship to the Mexicans in the newly purchased land as all of a sudden tens of thousands of Mexican nationals found themselves leaving within the United States border. That's why it is often said that the first Mexicans to be part of the United States didn't cross the border, instead, the border was the one that crossed them. They literally found themselves in the U.S. because of the border line.

Up to 100,000 individuals who were living in the U.S. after the annexation became full citizens. The Hispanics in New

Mexico and California were loyalists and did not play a major role in the Mexican-American War or identifying with the regime in Mexico City. When they were offered the choice to go back to their mother land or remain and become full citizens, a majority opted to stay until large numbers of Americans arrived and most were just seen as Mexicans.

In California, initially 10,000 chose to remain behind in 1848, but soon they were snowed under by a wave of new comers consisting of hundreds of thousands of immigrants to the state who basically became indiscernible to the Anglos.

The treaty had promised that those owning land in the newly attained territory would be given full protection for their property just like it would happen to citizens of the United States, however, many former citizens of Mexico lost their claims in lawsuits before federal and state courts. In other areas mostly California, the Hispanic residents were besieged by the increasing population of Anglo-settlers who hurried to Northern California as a result of the California Gold Rush only decades later for the Hispanic miners to be driven out of their camps by Anglo-miners who also barred non-Anglos from testifying in court.

When Did the USA Start Bringing and Recruiting Immigrants from The South?

The United States has always been a destination of both freedom and opportunity for millions of people around the world. Immigration has served as an essential element of social and economic development in the United States as it has relied on a constant flow of newcomers to diversify the society and boost the economy. However, during times of unrest and economic strains anti-immigrant sentiments often come about.

From the beginning of the 1890s, new industries started sprouting in the Southwest of the U.S. especially in mining and agriculture, which attracted laborers who were Mexican immigrants. The Mexican revolution in 1910-1920 then rapidly increased the number of immigrants to the United States. This prompted the U.S. to outsource for labor.

Post colonialism immigration began when Mexico and the U.S. got in to a boundary dispute that brought about the famous Mexican-American War. And the Treaty of Guadalupe sited before.

The treaty offered a blanket naturalization to the estimated 75,000 to 100,000 former citizens of Mexico who made the decision to remain at the north of the new border at the end of the war between the U.S. and Mexico.[73]

The other immigrants to enter U.S. soil were 10,000 Mexican miners who came to California during the Gold

Rush. During the 19th century, immigration was relatively low averaging about 3,000 to 5,000 persons per decade between the years of 1840 and 1890. However, things changed dramatically at the beginning of the following century. Due to economic development in the West of America, which was caused by the expansion of the regional rail system in the 1870s and 1880s, there was a need for laborers. The supply for labor from Asian nations had drastically reduced following a number of restrictive immigration laws, which began in 1882. The U.S. then started outsourcing for laborers in Mexico with the increased demand for labor in basic industries such as agriculture, construction, mining and transportation, particularly in construction and maintenance of railroads. Attracted by economic advancement in the northern border, at least 100,000 Mexicans migrated to the U.S. by 1900.[74]

However, in 1910, the Mexican Revolution resulted in an increase in Latin American migration. War refugees and political exiles fled to the United States to run away from the ongoing violence. Most Mexicans left their rural areas to source for employment and stability; as a result, Mexican migration to the United States grew rapidly as the numbers went from around 20,000 migrants per year in the 1910s to about 50,000-100,000 per year in the 1920s — bringing the estimated number of Mexican immigrants to about 639,000.

By 1930, the total number of Mexican-origin population was at least 1.5 million with the largest group concentrated in the states of California, Texas, and Arizona and another significant number working in industrial fields in the Midwest metropolitan, mostly areas of Chicago, Detroit, and Indiana.[75]

During the great depression, an estimate of 350,000-500,000 Mexican immigrants and their children were pressured or forced to leave the country in a mass ethnic cleansing campaign coordinated by local, state, and federal officials. However, the Mexican migration pattern quickly resumed after the United States joined the Second World War in 1941.

After encountering a massive farm labor scarcity as a result of taking people to war and repatriating others, the U.S. lobby groups persuaded the Federal government to approach Mexico about the possibility of implementing an emergency labor agreement. Mexican government officials were humiliated by the suffering of their nationals and children working in the US, therefore they were reluctant at first to enter into the agreement. The Mexican government secured guarantees from the U.S. officials that saw that their workers would be provided transportation to and from Mexico, decent food, a fair wage, and housing. Basic human rights protection was to be offered, therefore upon this, the two governments signed the Emergency Farm Labor Agreement in 1942.[76]

The acquiring of Latin American workers was given the name the Bracero program, the Spanish colloquial name for manual laborers. It had long term effects and one of them was re-opening the southern border to Mexico labor and also reinstituting the use of large numbers of immigrant workers to the U.S. economy for the first time since the Depression. The dynamics of this program remained averagely functional through the war years with an approximate of 70,000 laborers working in the country each year during the war.

In 1939, the number had plummeted to 113,000 and then an average of 200,000 per year between 1950 and 1954. When the program was in its peak years between 1955 and 1960, the average number of laborers was more than 400,000 predominately from Mexico. These Mexican-origin laborers were also supplemented by a smaller number of Jamaicans, Bahamians, Hondurans, and Barbadians. At the time of termination of the program, closely to 5 million contracts had been given out.[77]

The Bracero program helped to institute an increment of both sanctioned and unsanctioned migration to the U.S. from Mexico. Due to reinforced communication networks between contract laborers and their friends and loved ones in their places of origin in Mexico, the rising population of Mexicans was attaining considerable knowledge regarding labor market conditions, migration routes to the north of the border and also employment opportunities. Evidently, the number of Mexicans who legally migrated to the United States rapidly increased in the 1950s and 1960s from 219,000 in the 1950s to about 459,000 in 1960s.

The program also encouraged a drastic increase in unauthorized migration of Mexicans whose aim was improving their material condition and livelihood by moving to the U.S. as wages there were seven to ten times higher than wages paid in Mexico. Tens of thousands of Mexicans— almost all of them males and of working age, chose to go against the formal labor contract process but instead opted to cross the border. The number of unauthorized immigrants rose from an astounding 91,000 in 1946 to almost 200,000 in 1947 and more than 500,000 by 1951.[79]

Immigration Has Always Been a High Priority for Many Caucasian Republican Voters

The current U.S. immigration law is very complex and confusing in regard to how it works as it has changed throughout history. Through recent censuses on recurring issues to Republican voters, immigration was given the top most priority as an important issue. In 2013, the U.S. senate passed a comprehensive reform bill intended to make it probable for undocumented immigrants U.S. to gain legal status and ultimately citizenship. It would also increase security at the border by adding up to 40,000 border patrol agents. The bill also suggested the formation of a point-based immigration system that would enhance talent based immigration. In the legislation, new visas were proposed which included W-visa intended for lower skilled workers and a visa for entrepreneurs. The bill also entailed a $1.5 billion program to create youth jobs that favor prospective legal immigrants who are already residing in the U.S.

Currently, a solid majority of 66 percent Hispanic voters believe that passing the new immigration bill as proposed in 2013 is extremely important, this is up by 6 percent as compared to when the bill was first proposed. Among Latino registered voters, foreign born more likely than the U.S. born say that passing the new immigration bill is extremely important by a margin of 77 percent to 61 percent. Similarly, 76 percent of Spanish-dominant Latinos and 71 percent of bilingual Latinos are more likely than 55 percent of their English dominant counterparts to say that passing the new immigration reform bill soon is extremely important.

Latino registered voters have differences in assigning blame as to who is the cause for the lack of progress on the new immigration bill. According to educational attainment levels, about 51 percent of Latino registered voters with at least some college education, blame the Republicans in Congress for the delay in passing new immigration legislation, whereas, 30 percent blame President Barack Obama, and 18 percent blame the Democrats in Congress.

Similarly, 35 percent of Latino registered voters who have no high school diploma place their blame to the Republicans in Congress, while 46 percent of them blame President Barack Obama and 32 percent blame the Democrats in Congress. Among almost all Latino adults, 40 percent of Democrats in Congress and President Barack Obama are highly likely to be blamed for the stalling of the immigration legislation as 40 percent blame falls on the Republican Congress. There are no significant differences found between those born in the U.S. and foreign-born Latinos on this matter.

While there has been very little progress on passing the new significant immigration legislation, still the number of unauthorized immigrants deported and those apprehended at the border continues to grow. In 2013, more than 438,000 immigrants were deported, and an increased number of apprehensions at the U.S. Southwest border are of non-Mexican immigrants with a number of them being Central American unaccompanied minors.

When Latinos were asked about what the priority should be in dealing with Immigration in the United States, 84 percent of the registered voters say that creating a pathway to citizenship for undocumented immigrants should be a top priority with a 46 percent as important as better border security with 38 percent. The lesser percent of the registered voters with 14 percent believe that better border security is the top priority. Only 23 percent of the U.S.

adult general public consider the roadmap to attaining citizenship as a main concern. About 33 percent of the same prioritize better border security and enforcement as compared to 10 percent of Latino adults.

Is It Racism or Political Strategy or Both

In regards to racism, most Republican Caucasian voters indirectly move around in circles while some fear to be taken out of context. However, most republicans feel that their concerns on immigration are vilified. They argue third point's issues such as security matters and economic while some say it's unfair that illegal immigrants get some privileges such as healthcare and welfare without having to necessarily work for them.

As a political strategy, Republican presidential candidates are faced with tough questions from Republican Caucasian voters as to how they will handle the issue of immigration if elected. They characterize their concerns with illegal immigration as a case of national security, economic concerns and fundamental fairness. Most believe that immigrants working in the U.S. illegally drive down wages and benefits despite the fact that originally, most U.S. citizens are immigrants from other places.

Most Republican Caucasian voters have listed immigration as one of their major concerns stating that the economic wellbeing and security of the United States should be considered as high priority. Therefore, most Republican candidates use this as a campaigning tool especially during election years so as to push forward their own agendas.

How Many Undocumented Workers Are from Latin-America?

Latin-American undocumented workers mainly constitute of illegal immigrants and by 2012, about 52 percent were from Mexico, 15 percent from Central America, 6 percent from South America while the rest came from Asia, Caribbean, Europe and Canada. By 2014, about 5.6 million unauthorized immigrants from Mexico lived in the USA. This declined by about a million immigrants since 2007. Studies in recent years have shown that Mexicans make up to about 49 percent of unauthorized immigrants in regard to the general overall amount of immigrants. Among undocumented Mexican immigrants aged 16 and above, close to 19 percent worked in construction and about 13 percent worked in a wide range of businesses.

According to the 2008 census, the labor force for the USA was made up of 154 million people, this estimated 8.3 million Latin-America undocumented workers. Among states, the proportion of undocumented workers vary widely especially with the states that have high number of Latin Americans. For example, labor force in Arizona,

California and Nevada is roughly more than 10 percent but less than 2.5 percent in other states, especially those in the Midwest and Plains states. Most of these workers are unlikely to get those skilled jobs, but their share of some of these occupations has grown through the years.

What Is Their Economic Power and Contribution?

It has been proven that illegal immigrants are important to the USA economy as well as vital to certain industries including agriculture. Without the undocumented immigrant population, the workforce for Texas would plunge by 6.3 percent while the gross state product would fall by 2.1 percent. The USA Department for Agriculture states that half of the hired workers employed in the USA's crop and agriculture sector were authorized with a majority of them coming from Mexico. They also warned that any potential immigration reform legislated could have a significant impact on the USA fruit and vegetable industry.

On the National Milk Producers Federation's perspective in 2009, retail milk would increase by 61 percent if the government was to eliminate its immigrant labor force. The truth of the matter being, if a substantial number of undocumented farm workers were to be deported, there would be a tremendous labor shortage.

The department of labor reports that there are 2.5 million farm workers in the U.S. and about 53 percent of these farm workers are illegal immigrants, however, growers and labor unions put the figure close to 70 percent.

Reasons for Latino Immigration

The Bracero Program

Bracero is a Spanish word meaning manual laborer or one who works using his arms. Bracero program entailed a sequence of diplomatic agreements and laws that were put forward on the 4th of August in 1942. This was when the U.S. along with Mexico put their signs on the Mexican Farm Labor agreement. The agreement guaranteed basic human rights, which included sanitation, an adequate shelter, food, and a minimum wage amounting to 30 cents per hour. The agreement saw the importation of short-term contract laborers to supply workers during times of war as a momentary war-related clause. The agreement was extended with the migrant labor agreement, which helped set the parameters for the Bracero program until it was terminated in 1964.

Economic Crisis in Latin America

This was also known as the lost decade during the time when Latin America was in foreign debt exceeding their earning power, thus, weren't able to repay. In the 1960s and 1970s, many Latin American countries, mainly Brazil,

Argentina and Mexico had borrowed huge amounts of money from international creditors for the purpose of industrialization and especially for infrastructure programs. During this time, these countries had declining economies so the creditors continued providing loans.

When the world's economy went into recession between 1970s and 1980s, during that time, oil prices sky-rocketed creating an economical breaking point for most countries in the region. As interest rates increased in the USA and Europe, debt payments also increased making this harder for the countries in debt to pay back their debtors. A deterioration in the exchange rate with the U.S. dollar also meant that the Latin American governments owed huge quantities of their national currencies and lost their purchasing power as well. The debt crisis of 1992 resulted in stagnated economic growth and a tremendous decline of income. Due to the need to reduce importations, unemployment rose to high levels and inflation reduced the buying power of the middle classes. In response to the crisis, most Latin-American inhabitants moved to the USA in search of better opportunities and employment.

NAFTA

NAFTA stands for Northern American Free Trade Agreement and was a program that was supposed to take care of immigration and make Mexico rich through creation of employment incentives. It was supposed to reduce the number of unauthorized Mexican immigrants entering the U.S. each year, however, in the years that followed, there was a substantial increase of illegal immigrants from Mexico into the U.S.

The U.S. government all along has been protecting farmers since 1930s against unpredictable hardships including bad weather and economic depression. Today, the subsidies going to agriculture and the insurance cost burden the U.S. taxpayers where they have to pay $20 billion every year, according to U.S. Government Accountability Office. There has been a lot of scrutiny in recent years concerning this support where it is thought that the money goes to giant agribusiness and millionaire farmers and not the small family farms, which are seeking to stay afloat.[80]

In 2014, Congress initiated agricultural support programs that eliminated the controversial system involving direct payment to farmers and instead, it provided farmers with crop insurance subsidies. However, opponents of such moves feel that the government still continues to provide costly income support that is not even needed in the industry, in the first place. Other people in support of the programs feel that they are necessary because they provide the necessary protection to the population against high food prices and food scarcity.

A professor serving at Montana State University in the departments of agricultural economics argues that farmers need to be let alone to stand on their own. While this may be the perception among the U.S. people, what about the implication to the issue of immigration?

Mexico and Latin-America can't compete with the $20 billion in subsidies offered by the U.S government to its farmers. Farm workers go to the USA to work as they are out of a job.

NAFTA, at the time of being signed had a lot of fanfare and great promises. However, the trade deal that was supposed to be a boon by helping regional trade has brought some unwanted effects. It hastened illegal immigration into the U.S. In the past before NAFTA, the Mexican government used to offer subsidies in corn. Corn is the staple for Mexicans as it is used to make foods like the tortillas. With the subsidy by Mexican government to its farmers, it kept the prices of crops like corn quite low as to help farmers stay in business. At the same time, it helped keep the tortilla price at low levels so that Mexican poor people could be able to eat it.

However, when NAFTA came into effect some two decades ago, it phased out tariffs with the intent of lowering costs and encouraging investment between Canada, U.S. and Mexico. Suddenly, the Mexican government ended its corn subsidy— quite too quickly.

On the other hand, the U.S. government continued to subsidize its farmers ensuring that the corn producers in the country are highly productive. Close to 75,000 Iowa farmers grew twice the corn that three million farmers in Mexico could grow at half of the cost. Soon, the Mexican market was flooded with corn from the U.S.

There was an influx of Mexican farm workers to the big cities as they left their countryside. Millions of other Mexicans crossed over to enter the U.S. illegally. The big wave of illegal immigration to U.S. from Mexico began in 1980s and it strongly picked up soon after NAFTA. This is something that had been predicted before the agreement was signed.

In fact, the Mexico-U.S. immigration can be said to be more like a 20-year hump contrary to a 10-year hump because from the time the trade agreement was signed, was when we had a huge number of immigrants cross to U.S. The 20-year bulge in illegal immigration contributed to huge militarization of the border as well as millions Mexican immigrants living underground in the U.S.

Crime and Terror

Organized criminal groups have proliferated in the recent years and vary from street gangs to drug trafficking organizations to military mafias who take advantage of weak government institutions so as to control a particular physical territory. They also thrive where new criminal economies have emerged and can easily diversify their own agendas. They also use violence and the threat of violence so as to achieve their goals whether political or criminal.

Latin-America is among the most violent regions in the world today, often registering as one of the most homicidal regions with four Central American countries. Throughout the region, extortion and complaints for kidnapping keep rising with some countries having homicide rates that would qualify as epidemic. The United Nations Development Program reported that 460 people a day suffer from sexual violence therefore causing displacement and immigration.

Not all illegal immigrants are entering the U.S. to seek for job opportunities. Some are fleeing laws in their countries to seek refuge in the U.S. after being implicated in criminal activities. Others are entering the U.S. to continue their malicious activities of advancing practices like drug trafficking.

From Mexico and other countries in South America, organized crime threatens to kidnap or kill family members and families have to go north looking to hide from crime. While these may enter the U.S. illegally, on the other hand, branding them as illegals may not be the right thing. These are people fleeing from attacks or possible homicides from gangs. These may be seen as refugees fleeing wars however, this time it is war by organized group of gangs. The main question that arises is; should they be considered political refugees instead of illegals or undocumented?

If they find their way illegally, they may be labeled as undocumented illegal immigrants, but if they are granted permission to seek hideout, they can be labeled as political refugees because the governments in their countries have failed to guarantee them security.

Mason Dixon Line

I met Miguel Kelly in Mexico City during a business trip. We sat elbow to elbow in a crowded table between walls at a Chili's restaurant just outside a convention. After introductions and friendly conversation I told Kelly that I was writing a book titled Latino Vote touching on American politics. Our conversation quickly changed to politics, immigration and history.

Miguel Kelly, is an American citizen born and raised in Mexico of American parents. The parents went to Mexico as missionaries. Kelly is a real life rocket scientist in the U.S. and studied in Stanford University.

I asked his views on immigration especially on undocumented workers in the U.S. I thought he could bring an interesting view since he's an American living in Mexico. And, before he could give me his views about the question, he asked me if I have read about the Mason Dixon Line. "I know what it is, but maybe you're going to surprise me?" I said. He did.

"I want to answer your questions based on the use of the Mason Dixon Line to separate slave states from non-slave states" said Miguel Kelly.

The South wanted to expand the territory of states that had slaves to increase the economy and augment the members of Congress to have influence in politics. They wanted to maintain slaves in the South with political influence but they couldn't because there were more people and more members of Congress in the North. What they thought was to first establish a state in Mexico and then to expand the US territory all the way to the west coast of California and dominate the country with slaves and grow the economy while having a majority in the Congress. This would protect their right as slavers for in the future. This one move would grow the South's wealth by keeping a slave workforce while at the same time ensuring political protection based on lawmaking.

The U.S. proceeded to take over the northern territory of Mexico by invading it and this is what we know now as the modern U.S. with all the states.

Kelly's point on immigration was simple and powerful. The US took over Mexican territory illegally. Then, it called its citizens illegals. Now it's calling immigrants illegals.

In invading Mexico, The USA broke every international law. It marched all the way to the capital in Mexico City and made the president sign a treaty by force, giving away more than half of Mexico to the USA.

"We're hypocrites" said Miguel Kelly. "Calling people illegals and pointing fingers. We did worse" he continued.

Talking about the Mason Dixon Line, Miguel Kelly touched some on the annexation of Texas. It started with U.S. citizens (planted by the US government) going to Texas and asking the Mexican government if they could live in Texas and rent the property. However, under the Mexican constitution, they could not do this because they were American citizens, so they decided to denounce their American citizenship and become Mexicans in order to comply with the law of the land. Now, these new Mexican citizens who had denounced their American citizenship wanted to separate themselves from Mexico to be an independent state. So in reality, that was not what they wanted. It was all a foul play by the U.S. to take over Texas and therefore, the US started a war.

Miguel Kelly's point is well taken. Immigration is not as simple as legal and illegal. It's about who makes the law and when they make it. It's easy to still, then change the law to make that property your own and prosecute you if you trespass.

History of Mason Dixon Line

In the years between 1763 and 1967, Jeremiah Dixon and Charles Mason surveyed and marked many of the boundaries running between Maryland, Pennsylvania, and another three counties that later on became Delaware. The survey was commissioned by Calvert and Penn families and was intended to sort out things on the boundary dispute that existed for a long time. This provides a reference point concerning the history of this region.

James Bradley was a royal astronomer and he recommended that Jeremiah Dixon and Charles Mason complete the survey of the boundary. Mason was an assistant of the Bradley's observatory and also an Anglican widower bearing two sons. Dixon on the other hand was a skilled surveyor coming from Durham and was a Quaker bachelor though he had been ousted because he was unable to abstain from drinking liquor.

Both Mason and Dixon had put out to sea together in 1761 moving from Sumatra and making it to the Cape of Good

Hope were they were to record the transit of Venus across the sun in a bid to help calculations by Royal Society of distance between sun and Earth using parallax. The task in America was to get the exact tangent line in north from the center point of the trans peninsular line all the way to the twelve-mile arc as well as survey the boundary east-west five degrees westward in a line of latitude making its way fifteen miles on the south of southernmost part of Philadelphia. This was a great technological milestone of that century.

Both Dixon and Mason arrived in Philadelphia on November 15, 1763 in a time when there was a lot of tension. The Seven Years War brought too much tension and that had spilled over to touch on North America such as the French and Indian Wars. [81]

Even as the making of the boundaries by Mason and Dixon continued, there was hostilities and fighting. Indians were almost completely displaced from eastern states. There was a national debate that focused on abolition of slavery. A debate on whether new states joining the Union needed to be free or slave states continued.

In 1820, the Missouri Compromise designated that Mason and Dixon west line become the national divide separating the "slave" and "free" states within the east part of the Ohio River. This line now gained a great significance.

The 1776 the state constitution of Delaware had abolished the importation of slaves. The state legislation stopped exportation of slaves in 1797 when it declared exported slaves to be automatically free.

By 1790, the population of Delaware state was 15 percent black and of these blacks, only 30 were free. The others were slaves. By 1820, the census showed that Delaware had about 78 percent free blacks and by 1840, percentage of free blacks in that state went up to 87 percent.

Immigration Programs and Laws

Amnesty Programs and Immigration Laws

Immigration laws are national policies, which control the experience of immigration to their country. Immigration laws governing foreign citizens may be regarded as a nationality law that presides over the legal status of persons in issues like citizenship.

Amnesty is derived from the Greek word amnestia, which means forgetfulness; it is defined as the pardon granted by a government to class of people subject to trial but have not yet been convicted. It includes more than just pardoning to the degree that it wipes out all legal remembrance of the offence— so it is used mostly to give and express freedom as well as denote a time when prisoners can go free.

1: The Immigration Reform and Control Act of 1986

It is also known as the Simpson Mazzoli Act and was
enacted by Congress in response to the large and rapidly
growing population of undocumented immigrants in the
U.S. The final bill due to a staged negotiation between
those who considered having a fresh start for
undocumented immigrants by granting them permanent and
legal residence and those who strove to lessen illegal
immigration.

The IRCA amnesty program was inclusive for two main
categories of illegal immigrants. The first category was for
those who could show that they had resided in the U.S.
continuously since January 1st 1982. The second category
included immigrants who had worked as agricultural
workers for not less than 90 days in the period between
May 1st 1985 and May 1st 1986. The IRCA was signed
into law by President Ronald Reagan on November 6th
1986.

The law was drafted due to the increased number of illegal
immigrants and employers knowingly hiring undocumented
immigrants. This was able to be reduced as financial
sanction and other penalties were introduced for those
employing illegal immigrants. These regulations
promulgated under the Act introduced the 1-9 form to

ensure all employees gave documentary proof of their eligibility to qualify for employment in the United States.

2: Immigration and Nationality Act

This was a temporary rolling Amnesty for 578,000 illegal immigrants. Section 245(i) was constituted in immigration law after the Congress passed the Commerce, Justice State Appropriations Bill. In nearly all cases, a person must be an illegal immigrant so as to benefit from section 245(i).

The two major kinds of illegal immigrants to benefit from this were; those who got into the country illegally while the second category were those who got into country legally with a valid visa but failed to honored its terms and conditions. The Immigration Act of 1990 was a national reform of the Immigration and Nationality Act of 1965. It was signed into law by President George H.W. Bush on November 29th 1990. It increased the total for the overall migration and allowed 700,000 immigrants to come to the U.S. per year between 1992-1994 and 675,000 per year after that.

3: Section 245(i) Extension Amnesty of 1997

President Bill Clinton signed continuing resolutions twice to extend the expiring date of section 245(i)— the first resolution extended the deadline up to 23rd of October 1997 and the second one extended the deadline to 7th of

November 1997. Section 245(i) was then further extended to 14th of January 1998 by Congress.

4: Nicaraguan Adjustment and Central American Relief Act

It is an amnesty meant for some particular group of Cubans and Nicaraguans. It is a de facto amnesty created for certain Guatemalans, Salvadorans, and Eastern Europeans. The original bill that was introduced in the House and the Senate in 1976 would have benefited only some Guatemalans, Salvadorans, and Nicaraguans. Inclusions of Eastern Europeans and Cubans were done later on to appease the anti-communists sentiments echoed by some members of Congress.

Concurrently those who were opposing the amnesty were trying to bargain for a requirement that the number of undocumented immigrants who were given legal residence as per NACARA be taken away from legal immigration ceilings. Nonetheless, they only managed to get minor reductions particularly in the unskilled worker and others like those in lottery categories. The language bill was added as an amendment to the appropriations bill in order to do away with a never ending debate regarding the cost as well as benefits of such amnesty. Nicaraguans and Cubans who had lived in the United States illegally since 1995 were given legal resident status as stipulated under NACARA provided that they applied not later than the 1st of April,

2000. During the ten-year impact of the NACARA Amnesty on the U.S., the estimated population growth was about 966,480.

On the 7th of January 2004, President George W. Bush, for the first time, addressed immigration policy by proposing his first formal request to Congress. The proposal included the introduction of a short term worker program to cater for newcomers as well as the immigrants who were at that time residing in the U.S. without legal documentation or authorization. He explained that such a reform was needed in order to minimize on the potential of national security threat of having more than 8 million unidentified and undocumented illegal aliens in the United States. He also emphasized that the proposed reforms would not only aid in prevention of future exploitations of immigrants and human trafficking but also protect the wages of all workers.

President George W. Bush's proposal included that:
- The program was to be open to new workers applying from their home country and to undocumented immigrants currently living in the U.S.
- The number of Visas available under the temporary worker's program be determined by the number of available jobs
- The new short-lived visas would only be valid for a period not exceeding three years. It however, would be renewable to an unnamed number of times

- Temporary workers under the new program would be able to leave and reenter the country at will
- The proposed temporary workers program would be non sector
- The said Visas would be portable and not tied to a particular job as all immigrants would have the right to change jobs
- Undocumented immigrants applying from within the U.S. would be required to prove that they are currently employed and pay a fee
- Immigrants applying from abroad would require an offer of employment from a U.S. employer.

These are just a few of the suggested reforms, which received many positive reactions even though a majority of people including legislators, immigration experts and advocates doubted whether it could work.

PART II

LATINOS FACTS AND FICTION

The American Wall: Drugs, Aliens and Tunnels

Is the wall working? Are we keeping drugs, terrorists and undocumented workers out? All research points to failure.

Being tough on drugs might get you votes, but it's a waste of time, money, and directly proportionate to drug cartel profits. The more the U.S. spends on incarcerating drug users and fighting the supply of drugs, the more money they make to the drug cartels. In the book Narconomics (PublicAffairs February 23, 2016), author Tom Wainwright concludes that supply chain intervention of any kind only increases profits of drug cartels.

Tom Wainwright explains how supply is not curving when drug prices go up. Prices might go up if it's more difficult to get drug into the country. In this case cartels make more profit. If you capture or burn crops from farmers attempting to disrupt the supply of an illegal drug, it only affects the farmer, as the cartel doesn't own the land or the crops. The local cartel continues to buy the crop for the same price. The author compares this to Wal-Mart. If Wal-Mart is your largest buyer and you had a rough year in production, you don't raise the price, you either sell at the agreed price and take the hit, or go out of business. Furthermore, Wainwright explains how incarceration of drug users in the U.S. only helps with the recruitment of new employees for the cartels. If a young man goes to prison on drug use charges he'll need protection from a gang to survive against hardened criminals. In turn, he has to pay back the gang by joining, and working for them.

The wall helps the drug cartels, hitting supply chain helps cartels, and imprisoning users helps them recruit new members. Prevention is not working either. If all of this don't work, what does? Rehabilitation seems to be the only return on investment that's working. It's not sexy, but it works. How about legalizing drugs? This will put the cartels out of business according to Wainwright.

"It has been all wrong"
Said the U.S. Drug Czar Michael Botticelli on a 60 Minutes interview when asked if our drug policy is working. The past forty years of drug enforcement are wrong.

Securing the US border has always been a high political priority. Now the word terrorism is included with drugs and illegal aliens, further giving reason for spending money and building higher walls.

How will history view The American Wall? Will we look back at this the same way we look at the Berlin Wall? Or as not so proud moments in US history that started with ownership of slaves that later converted into racism? Or will we simply see it as a normal action of protectionism?

In my travels through Germany and Western Europe several friends asked me about The American Wall, and I had the opportunity to show several of them the wall when they traveled to San Diego, California. On one occasion I crossed the border with my friend Christian Hoffman on one of his trips from Germany. We drove along the border wall and saw crosses fixed on the wall on the Mexican side. "What is that?" he asked. "One cross for every body found," I told him. We continue driving and the crosses didn't stop. You could see one after another after another nailed to the military style steel wall erected to keep the unwanted out. "How many crosses in total?" he asked. "There are seven thousand crosses. All died crossing the border," I told him. He looked at me seriously and incredulously. "I don't understand," he said, "This has to be one of the worst human rights violations of the country."

As we drove we could see people gathering alongside the wall looking through cracks and holes. "What are they doing?" he asked. I explained how they are going to jump the fence and avoid border patrol. My friend had another jaw dropping expression. "Why would someone do that?" he asked. "Exactly!" I answered.

According to *The Smithsonian Magazine* October 1st article more than 6,000 immigrants have died at the US border from the year 1998 to 2014 citing a report from the International Organization for Migration. To put this into perspective the Berlin Wall was protagonist to 138 deaths from 1961 to 1989 according to the Berlin Wall Memorial. Further investigation on the American Wall revealed that the numbers can go up to 7,000 deaths. The number is based on bodies found, not actual deaths. There is no current investigation of how many people actually died. Bodies could still be in the desert, buried, or retrieved by family members.

If Walls Could Talk

If the American wall could talk, it would probably have two messages:

1. *Beyond this wall is the American Dream, life, liberty and the pursuit of happiness*

2. *Keep Out!*

The American Wall and fear of immigration or minorities has been a favorite of politicians new and old. Pointing to a minority is a very easy way to rally support to your cause. Especially when a percentage of the majority feels they are economically satisfied. "You lost your job? They are taking your job." "You don't have enough money? They are milking the welfare program." It's amazing to see this movement take place not only in the USA but in different countries. Genocides started the very same way all over the world. "You have problems? Blame it on them," evolved rapidly to "You have problems? Kick them out of the country," to "Kill all of them".

You may think killing Latinos or immigrants is a far cry from blaming them for all the woes of the country. It is not. When you see radicals take arms and patrol the border shooting immigrants, or the KKK endorsing a candidate because he's anti-Latino and the same candidate winning votes around the country you can start counting hands.

Violence against a minority doesn't start as violence. It always starts with a leader blaming that group for the nation's problems, then slowly gathering support until a tipping point is achieved. After this, sometimes but not always, a call to action is made to "get rid" of the minority group.

This is a very hard conversation to uncover. What surprises me is the arguments politicians have against immigrants, Latinos or Mexicans. Studying historical records, you can equate the same rhetoric and propaganda used by Mussolini and Hitler.

This type of racism can start anonymous or with votes for a candidate. This issue rings true to several of the Latinos I interviewed as well as for myself. I've received death threats, racist comments and the most vulgar and derogatory comments that you can imagine. So vile and insulting just thinking about them for the book makes me doubt their humanity.

Having a wall that is monitoring and limiting movement of people appears to be a ferocious violation of human rights and freedom of movement. Several people have been denied that chance to freely participate in legitimate trade and business with people from both countries due to imposition of this wall. The situation is even worse as the problem has not been curbed in any way and continues to bite as it was previously before the wall was erected.

The wall spells doom to the free movement of goods and services for the people from either country. This barrier that has the potential of destroying border relations between America and Mexico should not be allowed to continue.

America has always been in the forefront in championing human rights and building of the wall spells doom to basic human rights of the people affected by it. One intention of the wall is to curb drug traffickers and drugs access into America. This intention has gone further to affect farmers, traders, and the environment at large. Several private farms have been demarcated in parts of Texas where the wall is passing. This wall affects the movement of these people as they try to access their parts of lands that have been put out of their reach.

The transport system has also been dealt a blow as those whose land was demarcated have to follow a long route before reaching their destination. This may pose a new system of business whose aim is to leverage on their vulnerability to make profits. This is an exploitation of their rights which is not legal. Creating a system of exploitation harms the welfare of these people, who may be economically unstable. This is causing most people to incur a lot of expenses as they try to maneuver several hurdles they find on their way.

The wall limits an ideal environment for business to thrive as no business can thrive with a block in place. Mexico may feel isolated as it has been left with a heavy burden to carry. The menace of drug trafficking is a serious problem that is very much entrenched in Mexico. The menace needs to be tackled in a concerted effort to help curb the problem from the root cause.

When the drug trafficking issue is left to grow just within Mexico, it may blow out of proportion and even filtrate through the wall of America. This poses an even more major problem than what had been there before the building of the wall.

The wall has been a threat to the environment affecting wildlife and the natural flow of the ecosystem. The problem will expansively affect the wildlife where free movement of wild animals will be affected in a large way. Water is also affected where the flow from one point to another is interrupted. The ecosystem should be allowed to thrive freely without interference and this has been affected by the wall. Nature is important for the wellbeing of both humans and animals. The freedom of wild animals should be allowed for them to move from one point to another without regulations.

The issue can be used by politicians to gain political benefits as it bears a lot of magnitude in their lives. The pro Latinos can fuel the issue to gain political ground and influence their followers for their political advantage. Many people are opposed to the building of the wall, which has had detrimental effects to their lives. The issue may escalate with time and become a whirling wind in the politics of America. This may have an impact on the politics of America stirring a revolution in the political arena.

Asking the Wrong Questions

In a recent conversation with my friend Steve, a fifty-year-old Caucasian, a business man and investor, it opened my eyes on how the American Wall is perceived. He started the conversation with a question. "If we build a massive wall that makes it impossible to cross will they still go out to the dessert and try to cross it?" I looked at him for a moment incredulous to the question. "Wow!" I said to myself, "why is he asking this particular question?" I smiled and tried to answer to the question at hand, and bring forth what other questions could be in the mix.

"Yes, immigrants would keep coming. Especially the new wave of immigrants. The ones who are refugees escaping gangs in Central-America. Gangs that will steal their kids and make them join, or the ones from Mexico escaping violent crime. Some organized syndicates burn your house, kidnap your family, or torture the head of household until they get what they want. A wall, even a tall, thick, scary wall, will not stop them." I think he accepted the answer, or at least he took the time to think about it. Different immigrants have distinct motivations. For many it is work, but for others it's life and death.

The other questions that we should be asking are the logical ones, the ones that don't take the easy way out, or the vote-catching ones. Here are some of the questions:
"Why do we have a wall?"
"What was the original goal?"
"Is it fulfilling the goal?"
"What is the cost?"
"What is the return on investment?"
"Is it the best solution? What are other solutions?"

History of the American Wall

How did the wall start?

The modern US Mexico border wall started as an amendment to Border Protection, Anti-Terrorism, and Illegal Immigration Control Act of 2005, which was passed in the House. The amendment called for a plan to a mandatory fencing along the 698 miles of the 1,954 border. Later in 2006, George W. Bush signed into law the Secure Fence Act of 2006 that spearheaded the building of the wall. The U.S. Senate on September 29, 2006 confirmed the funding of the wall for a distance of 700 miles. The reason behind the building of the fence was to bar illegal immigrants from getting into United States. It was installed with sensors and cameras to spot those who illegally want to enter into the United States.

One of the original aims of the American Wall was also to control drug lords from trafficking drugs along the Mexico and southwestern United States of America. The menace of drug trafficking had become a major issue that had hardly hit the border between the United States and Mexico. There was a need to create a buffer that would deter the drug lords from transacting their business. The border also posed a threat in brewing a possibility of terrorism attacks in America. Terrorist would make their way into America and carry out attacks hence jeopardizing the security of the United States of America. The fence was constructed from San Diego through Arizona to Texas. It is 21-feet high to ensure that nobody easily slips past it. The wall is protected by the border patrol agents to ensure that there is no one who creeps into the water and enters the other side of the United States of America.[82]

Illegal migrants died while trying to cross the Sonora desert and there was a need to discourage them by erecting the wall. The wall's aim was to deter those who wanted to be crossing the border in pursuit of new places of making a living. The border had become a threat to both the security and the heritage of the nation.

Technology and new means of security had to be implemented in a bid to secure the country. The form of protection implemented did not auger well with most people, especially in Mexico. It has elicited a mixed reaction in America with most people supporting the building of the wall. The wall has been said to help reduce the number of people who have been trying to pass across the border into America.

Did we always have a wall dividing the USA and Mexico?

The wall did not always exist until the U.S. government realized that those who crossed the border posed a threat to the national security. The number of people crossing the border had been rising with each passing day and the drugs had been on the rise within America. There was a need to counter this and to prevent it from rising into a level that can get out of hand. This instigated the building of the wall to counter its effects, which were spreading at a dramatic rate.

Several millions of people had been crossing the border for a long time. In 2005, there were over 1,189,000 arrested while trying to cross the border into America. The wall had to be used to help monitor and control the passage of illegal migrants through the border. Several other people were being smuggled through the border and several of them died out of the harsh conditions during the time they were being transported.

Smuggling of goods and human beings made it necessary to build a barrier that would stop them from accessing America, and further discouraging them from thinking about crossing the border. A wall was thought to provide that mechanism that would create a buffer to help them reduce the number of those trying to cross.

Previously, there was no wall that existed between the USA and Mexico border, until the situation become very heated to an extreme that posed a danger to national security. Without the wall people could freely move across the border without being restricted by anyone. The openness of the border made it easy for people to take advantage of the situation by engaging in illegal businesses like drug trafficking. In a responsive move, the USA had to create a buffer to filter those crossing the border both to the USA and to Mexico.

The American Wall. What Is It For?

Easy question right? We're diving into the wall and what it does, how much it costs, but the simplest question is "what is it for?"

The American Wall is the wall dividing the USA and Mexico built originally to prevent illegal crossings of people and drugs into the USA.

Every answer to this question can be controversial if we explore the meaning. Immigration, drugs, and now terrorism and the trio of reasons used by politicians to defend the wall.

Is it working? No, it's not. On the contrary, it's helping cartels increase their profit. It's also increasing the price undocumented immigrants pay to get into the U.S. Increasing profit for Coyotes, or human smugglers. So much so that drug cartels are now getting into the business. Undocumented travelers pay as much as $5,000 per person to get into the USA.

To keep bad people out?

What are bad people? How many bad people come from Latin-American countries? Pro Latino activist will argue immigrants come to work, not to be bad. Far right activists have said Mexico sends the worst to the USA. This science fiction approach to politics is what really stirs anti-immigration and racist views towards immigrants. Let's look at the research: most legal and illegal immigrants come to the USA to work. Most find work and stay. We'll explore more about immigration trends in the book.

It is true several bad people were finding their way into America through this border, but another large number of people were after new employment in a bid to make their lives better. Several others moved to America as they tried to seek refuge as they escaped turmoil in their places of residents. Most children who moved to America were refuges who sought better living conditions than what they experienced back at their homes. Bad people are likely to exploit on the poor conditions of refugees hence denying them a chance to access help since the wall blocks both the legitimate and the illegal.

A mechanism should be put in place that deters illegal immigrants from masquerading as refugees since they are denying themselves a chance of getting assistance from the US government. Issuances of certificates should be conducted to those who legitimately come with the intention of getting assistance from the USA. The wall stands as a barrier to their hopes of accessing help making them even more hopeless and aggravating their pain even further.

Many of the immigrants travel over long distances braving harsh environmental conditions as they seek to find a place where they can be assisted and they believe that, that place is United States of America. Several of them travel and walk through deserts in an attempt to reach the border area to enter into America. They are astounded when they find a wall standing tall before them and denying them access to the only place where they believed was their last resort.

The wall denies legitimate traders in both sides of the border from engaging into business activities with one another. It affected many traders who were making a living from trading with those who were cut off by the wall. Travelling of traders was limited and they couldn't reap several economic benefits they used to get before the American Wall was built.

The perception that Mexico produces only bad people into the United States played a pivotal role in the decision to build the wall. But this is not always the case nor is it true; several important people have been produced by Mexico and they have made tremendous impact towards the development of America. The only problem with the United States is the widespread crime of drug and drug trafficking, which is a serious problem that the whole world should chip in to help instead of isolating Mexico.

Bad people cannot only be bred from one country and by saying that bad people in the United States of America only

originate from Mexico is ill-informed thinking. The wall
has dented Mexicans' economic gains in the name that
mostly bad people from America come from Mexico.
Another means of deterring bad people from entering
America should be adopted other than a wall that has
stacked a lot of misery on both human beings and wildlife.

Keep Immigrants Out

You would think a large wall would deter immigrants from
entering the country. That would be wrong. If an immigrant
crossed half the continent from South America to the US
border, aboard trains, avoiding immigration and police
from several countries, and have only a wall between
suffering and freedom, nobody could build a wall big
enough to stop them. Not only that, many immigrants that
are now illegally in this country arrived legally and
overstayed their permitted visit. A wall has no impact on
these immigrants.

In interviews with immigrants from Mexico and further
south I could not find a single case where the wall was a
deterrent from entering into the USA. Many of them were
caught and deported two, three, and up to five times before
they successfully crossed the border. Going back to their
country or town was not an alternative for them. They had
family and dreams waiting in the USA, and only despair
back home.

To keep drugs out

Yes, that's a great idea. We need to keep drugs out of the hands of users. However, there is absolutely no correlation between the wall and diminishing of drug trade. That's not the worst of it. The only thing that we can measure positively is the increase in profits to drug dealers. It's supply and demand. Drug users still get whatever drug they want, but now they have to pay more for them. What is disturbing is that drug users will use whatever they have to make sure they have bought the type of drugs they use. The wall will make the prices of drugs skyrocket but it won't prevent those who consume them from getting the drugs.

When the prices of drugs go high, the users may be tempted to engage in crime to get money that will fund them in buying the drugs. This will translate into an increase in the rate of crime in the United States. The USA turned to capturing drug lords in Mexico and the rest of Latin-America to address the problem. This too was a failure. It did not diminish either drug use or trade. What it did was to launch a civil war type of conflict in Mexico that left more than 164,000 people dead from 2007 and 2014 according to a July 27, 2015 KPBS Fronline article. It also spiked immigration into the USA. This time not only from undocumented workers and refugees, but from the upper Mexican leaving their country in fear of violence and kidnappings.

A wall doesn't keep drugs out. It's a simple invisible hand rule. This should be second nature in a capitalistic economy. The way you stop the supply of a product is by cutting the demand. If you cut the supply this increases the price, in turn the profits. The problem is that the appearance of being tough on drugs wins votes regardless of the effectiveness of the campaign. What does work is stopping demand, helping addicts to stop using drugs. Effective in practice, but not in politics.

According to the RAND Corporation for every dollar invested in drug treatment taxpayers will save $7.46.

Protect the country against terrorism

Another noble and worthwhile cause. We need to keep all terrorists foreign and domestic from attacking the country. The original American Wall was built before this theme became popular and expanded afterwards. The 9/11 terrorists entered the country legally. Terrorists from the Middle East have access to money, in turn can get visas and fly into the country. If they would fly into Mexico or other Latin-American countries they would have to present their Visa in Mexico, then proceed to enter into the USA. It is a much more difficult proposition.

Mexico as an example, has military, federal police and immigration checkpoints in different states and even at different airports. A potential terrorist flying to Mexico

City and then to a border town would have to avoid several checkpoints and x-rays not only entering, but exiting the airport. Some conducted by airport security, others by the military. If driving military checkpoints would search for weapons and check documents. Mexico is not a viable supply chain unless you have long rooted connections in the country for transportation, documentation, and you speak the language.

Price Tag of "Securing the Border"

Immigration and drug trade have been in the news a lot before the US, including protecting the border against terrorists into the equation. The country has spent over a trillion dollars fighting drugs and lost the battle long ago. "It has been all wrong," said the US Drug Czar Michael Botticelli on a 60 Minutes interview when asked if our drug policy is working. The country is investing in the wrong thing to a tune of one trillion dollars, and both supply and demand is increasing.

For a country that stresses our capitalistic nature, we sure spend a lot of time in anti-capitalistic ideologies. We see it with labor immigration, not allowing for competition for jobs. We see it in drug enforcement, focusing on building walls instead of using the invisible hand to take over and curve supply. If nobody wants drugs, the drug trade is gone — that is the nature of capitalism. On the other hand, by our own philosophy — it doesn't matter how much money we spend, how high we build walls and how many border patrol and drug enforcement officers we hire. Drugs are a product, and if there is demand for this product, somebody will take the risk to provide the supply. First semester college students learn this in Economics 101: Macroeconomics. Why do we need to spend a trillion dollars to understand it?

"Though on drugs" did not work in the last 40 years

If you're a fighter, then this is for you. Drug addiction is a disorder and also a crime as. The current treatment in the USA for this disorder is prison. Prisons are getting stuffed with more drug addicts every day and even if they get convicted, when they get out, very little changes about them and they still go back to taking drugs. If you want and are ready to fight this war on drugs then this piece is for you, can find help. Here is an excerpt of a report on the US Drug Czar, Michael Botticelli, as interviewed by Stott Pelley in 60 minutes.

Prisons are more than crowded, and a heroin epidemic outbreak is reaching new heights. It might be time for a change, nonetheless, we may not find another leader like Michael Botticelli — he is different. He isn't a cop, and luckily, he never went to jail.

The USA has used lots and lots of money for 40 years in the eradication of drug abuse, but up till now they have not accomplished much. Michael Botticelli, who is the US President's new Director of National Drug Policy is bent on bringing new changes and approaches on how to deal with drug abuse. Michael Botticelli was also an alcoholic who after his accident, got evicted from his apartment because he used all his money on alcohol and the judge gave him only two options to either get care for his drinking problem or get convicted— and that was his turning point.[83]

Many alcoholics go through this eviction, some lose their jobs because of the undying love they have for alcohol and drugs.

When interviewed by Scott Pelley, an anchor and managing editor serving in CBS Evening News and the correspondent of the program *60 Minutes*, Botticelli says that the new direction on drugs simply shows that the aged inactive ways and policies that are used in the fight against drug abuse have blundered. It may have been that the US government used a wrong approach in this war as the current outbreak of the heroin epidemic, increased number of prisoners jailed for drug crimes and the increase in number of Americans who use drugs and alcohol prove so.

Michael Botticelli also thinks that arresting these drug barons and users doesn't help in eradicating addiction, and even so, it has proven to be of very little help on the war on drugs. This also means using more money.

When asked what the people have gained from the outcome he says that it is not about drug addicts who are not self-disciplined and keep using drugs, but it's about the addiction, which is a brain disease. He says drug addiction influences the Cerebral Cortex, the part of the brain that regulates decision making, judgment, problem solving and controls of purposeful behaviors, consciousness and emotion.

He believes that *drug addicts should not be taken to prison like criminals* but should be treated as victims like what he did in Massachusetts as Director of Substance Abuse Services. His actions comprised of high school teens in recovery and expanding drug courts like in Washington D.C. where addicts can choose to be hospitalized other than going to prison so that the charges can be dropped. People may fear about releasing these people from prisons but it's all about treating the disorder and they would be reformed. And Michael is really pushing for reforms, which would also help reduce crime rates.

Just like the drug addicts, Botticelli has also struggled with addiction back in 1988, when he was a university administrator. When asked about it he says he drank to feel good about his insecurities as a kid in the struggle of growing up but the feeling didn't last. Many kids struggle out there in broken homes, alcoholic parents, and out of all these, they end up taking comfort in drugs too and forget they can do better, but the struggle isn't over yet. The feeling you get is always good but it's only going to make it worse and lead you to addiction.

Scott Pelley goes ahead and asks him about his accident and it is true that after the accident, he woke up handcuffed to a wagon or as some call it a "gurney". He is extremely grateful for walking into a church and on his first meeting he did not hesitate to admit he was an alcoholic and the people there were ready to assist. This gave him the motivation he needed to get rid of his addiction. This simply shows that anyone can overcome this disorder, so you have to own up and get help because you need it. Maybe this is your wakeup call, don't wait to meet an accident or get caught, you will be locked up and that's what you need to avoid.

Now that he has been free from the alcohol addiction for 27 years he commands $26 billion budget across 16 government agencies, which over half goes to drug enforcement.

When asked about what he thinks about those who argue that if the southern border is locked down (and there are many with this kind of perception), will it resolve the issue of drugs coming to the country from Mexico?

Botticelli replies by saying that it is overly simplistic to consider that a single strategy can change the focus and trajectory of drug use. Think of it this way, the heroin crisis we are experiencing in the nation started right here in America. One major driver of the heroin epidemic is the misuse of pain medications. What this means is that, if we have to deal with the problem of heroin use in the U.S. we have to reduce the amount of prescription drugs being used by patients.

Again, when asked about imprisoning drug addicts, he says just locking them up won't help solve the problem of drug abuse and addiction. He also goes ahead and explains that the prescription of pain medication, which mostly are opioids like heroin, should be reduced since its misuse is the main accelerator of heroin. Hence, the prescription of opioids has risen from 76 million in 1991 to 207 million today. Some people use these medications without even being aware of what they contain, but now you're enlightened— don't let these drugs get to your brain.

Still on the pain medication, Botticelli says America has a medical community that has slight coaching on pain, gets little training on addiction, and has been encouraging and continues to encourage the overprescribing of pain medications. Like, as we are told at Massachusetts General Hospital, where Dr. Leslie Kerzner treats opioids on newborns that are born addicted and uses morphine on them. The doctor goes ahead and explains that the number of pregnant mothers taking opioids seems to have gone up and without medication, they could have seizures.

Scott Pelley then asks Michael how an addict to prescription pain medication would find themselves on heroin. Michael explains that the prescription drugs act on the brain in the same ways as heroin, which is now easily and readily available in the streets of the USA.

Just like in other places, people die daily over drug overdoses. Michael also says that even police officers have lost their kids to a drug overdose, so it is not only civilians who use these drugs but everyone is affected. Michael has helped provide Naloxone to every Quincy officer. Naloxone is a nasal spray remedy used to counter overdose. Police Officer, Patrick Glynn confirms that Naloxone actually works within 45 seconds to a minute, then the victim would start moving, with quivering eyes, they actually sit up and talk. This is wonderful, and these officers are doing a great job responding immediately to these calls.

Under his administration, if an addict was caught on overdose, he would call 911 and would not be arrested for drug possession within the premises— this helped in saving more lives as more people called in and now 32 states have a similar 911 law and Naloxone is carried by more than 800 police departments.

Michael also states that most people who abuse drugs are always neglected until it gets to a worse phase and medical institutions have a major role to assist in pinpointing people in the early stages of their disorder. He refers it (addiction) as a disorder because changing the language drives the stigma that comes with addiction. He also wants people to speak up and face it with self-respect. Just in the same way he embraced his homosexuality, (now married to his husband David Wells for 20 years) he stood firm to get over alcohol addiction no matter how difficult it was.

He also tells Scott Pelley in his interview that addiction to legal drugs; alcohol and tobacco kill most Americans, over half a million a year. He believes that legalization of marijuana has made youths believe that it has no harm but it surely leads to addiction, poor academic performance, and in aggravating mental conditions linked to having a lower IQ. And, his big worry is that the marijuana industry seems to be quickly adapting the "big tobacco's" playbook.

Now that the marijuana industry is promoting sweetened edibles, and the tax revenue that will come from a prospering marijuana industry, Michael fears that talking all the states out of it would not be easy. As for his own, since he has experienced it, he knows that recovery from addiction isn't easy but it gets easier as you progress with the 12-step meetings, something he calls 'miraculous' and still attends them to date.

When asked about his advice to addicts watching the interview, he says that there's always hope no matter how hard or difficult it seems and there's also help in which helping people get over addiction makes him feel cool and proficient in his assignment.

I think with Botticelli's administration; his initiates would not only help enlighten the USA but also the world at large. Some of these policies, if put into practice and given time they would yield better results than the old ways as you've seen they are doing well.

So, what does this mean?

"After 40 years and a trillion dollars, the nation has little to show for its war on drugs"
60 Minutes
"It has been all wrong"

Michael Botticelli – US Drug Czar

The answer is simple; being tough on crime pays with votes, being tough on drugs pays with votes. Even if this policy doesn't work the politician is retired before we notice. It's up to the voters to make the change, not the politicians. According to the RAND Corporation for every dollar invested in drug treatment taxpayers will save $7.46. Economists agree that's the best investment of funds, so does the drug Czar and border patrol and drug enforcement agents I interviewed. "We have to stop the demand," every single one of them told me.

Drug Policy and Wasted Dollars

The U.S. has the largest consumption of drugs in the world but demand reduction strategies that have been proven are not being prioritized by the federal government. Education and treatment programs are more likely to improve health and public safety, and are also a way better investment as compared to incarceration and arrests. Seminal studies done find that taxpayers save $7.5 in societal costs for every dollar invested in the treatment of drugs.

The U.S. government spends more than $50 billion on the war on drugs every year and taxpayers are relied on to flip the bill. One in every 99 adults in the U.S. is imprisoned; this is the highest rate of incarceration in the world. Basic economic principles have been ignored and empirical evidence that funded the interdiction and law enforcement strategies have not been successful in the reduction of drug use but will continue to waste tax payers' dollars in fighting a losing battle.[84]

The rate of mass incarceration is increasing by the day and the United States financial sacrifices are all going down the drain despite all their well-resourced drug taskforces that help in the war on drugs. The supply and demand basic economic principle is an example, which has been distorted by the backward logic of the drug war.

Instead of addressing the issue of education strategies and treatments that could regulate drug demand, the federal government is busy pumping resources into interdiction policies and criminal justice that is not in the least bit helping the situation. Their main focus on the reduction of drug supply has not been successful in controlling organized crimes nor has it stopped any drug-related crimes.

Huge investments have not been consistent in the implementation of the set goals of reducing drug supply, production and consumption. It has instead increased the crime rate, which will result in substantial economic and social expenditures on health and crime that exceed the enforcement that took up billions of dollars. The expenditure on drugs is being considered wasteful since other important areas that require funding are being starved due to an enforcement that has not proven itself worthy but keeps draining the tax payer and government budget cuts are hitting the support of the needy as well as public services.

Regardless of the atrocious track record of failure, the spending of the drug enforcement has had an almost zero level of the study of value-for-money for both national and international levels. After literally wasting trillions over the past few decades, at a time such as this of global economic crisis, it is about time to make a meaningful account of the real cost of the war against drugs.

H.L. Mencken wrote a fervent plea in 1925 saying that prohibition has not only been a failure over the years but has in addition, created disturbingly serious problems in society. There is nothing but more drunkenness in the Republic at the moment, so as is crime. The government cost is greater and there is a highly diminished respect for the law.

Since the United States implemented prohibition, there has only been an increase in hard liquor intake, legal productions being taken over by organized crimes and increased rage towards the federal government. The U.S. has nothing to show since the war on drugs was declared four decades ago by Richard Nixon in 1971 but an all gone amount of $1 trillion.

So, What is the point?

The Point is that keeping drugs out is not working, the wall is not working and treatment and education is working. What should we do?

Not working in this case is an understatement. The country's drug policy is targeting minorities, incarcerating fathers for drug use and negating their children of a father in both education and economic contributions. It's also feeding the drug wars in Mexico and other Latin-American countries. Feeding them with money, weapons and demand. This in turn kills hundreds of thousands of people, destroys the economy and prompts the human collateral damage to immigrate to the USA.

The U.S. has the largest population of prisoners of about two million people behind bars. Most of those people are incarcerated because of violating drug laws. Young lives are being wasted because of this. When a company is failing in business, required measures are taken to solve the problem and not a continuation of using useless strategies that will cost ridiculous amounts of money and even worsen the situation. In this case of the war on drugs, the U.S. should look at what works and what doesn't by critically looking at data and real evidence.

The global drug trade would be a top economy country if it was to be one. The estimations of the United Nations show that the illegal drug trade is worth about $320 billion, which goes to show that there are over 200 million illegal drug users in the world and yet 90% of them don't even pose as a threat or even problematic. Studies show that the legalization of drugs would save the U.S. about $40 billion annually in administering these drug laws.

Clearly, drug laws have not reduced the use of drugs. Banning the use of these drugs does not stop people from consuming them; it instead increases the number of people breaking the law. If anything, the use of drugs has intensified over the years. The law now has a reputation of arresting the drug dealer but ends up leaving the addiction behind. As much as they insist that there would have been a much bigger problem if there were no laws against drugs, that wouldn't stop a consumer from consuming. The laws are there to be broken.

Smoking of marijuana and using acid have been practiced since 1970 and soldiers still come back home to their families when hooked on heroin. Richard M. Nixon says "for us to fight and defeat this enemy, we have to wage a new all-out offensive". At that time, the budget he presented was for about $100 million. Now it has bumped up all the way to $15 billion… which is 30 times more than the initial Nixon budget, which is a major inflation.

What Is All this Money Used for?

Over $20 billion is used to invade and arrest drug gangs in their own home countries. The U.S. spent about $6 billion in Columbia to fight trafficking but instead, it moved to Mexico and so did the violence and Coca cultivation. About $33 billion was used in the "Just say No" marketing program that sends messages to the youth, but have not helped since the Centers for Disease Control and Prevention give reports of increased cases of overdose.

About $121 billion is used to make arrests of millions of drug users who are nonviolent, most of who are arrested for the possession of marijuana. This does not even help the situation since statistics show that jail time only increases drug addiction. Close to $450 billion is used to lock up the federal prisoners. Last year, half of the prison population was occupied by drug offenders.

Aside from the above mentioned expenditures, drugs are costing the nation in many other ways. The system becomes overburdened and there is a strain on the healthcare system. This costs about $215 billion annually.

Economists in Harvard University say that the only thing taxpayers gain from all this is just an increase in homicides and increase of drug consuming youth. The policies we have currently are not helping in the reduction of drug use, but are instead just costing the nation a fortune. It has always been debated if the enforcement of law will really help solve the drug problem.

Mike Gravel, who is the Alaska senator said, "This is an ongoing tragedy that has cost us a trillion dollars and look what has happened, our jails are loaded and our countries like Columbia and Mexico have been destabilized".

Since 1970, the U.S. border has been effectively sealed to block the incoming of drugs by use of drones, sniffer dogs, patrols, several check points, motion detectors, cameras and even 1,000 miles of steel beam was put up with heavy mesh and concrete walls stretching from California to Texas, but have not even stopped the drugs. There are about 20 tons of heroin, 330 tons of cocaine and 100 tons of methamphetamine that are sold in the U.S. every year and all have been brought in through the borders. The justice system has been overwhelmed by the arrested dealers and most prosecutors have refused to file charges against 7,500 drug cases in the past year. That is an estimated 1 out of every 4 drug cases. These prosecutors lack enough evidence to arrest these Mexican gangs once the United States hands over some of these cases to them. These suspects then become deported, acquitted or even released. The U.S. government is not able to keep track of what happens to all of them. Investigators in Mexico will at times fail in collecting evidence and if they do, they end up being assassinated by some of these traffickers.

Suspects are usually beaten up by underpaid and frustrated police to force a confession and when they don't get anything, judges will turn a blind eye on the case and the suspects are released in enragement. However, the stakes are still very high and the issue cannot be ignored since this is the lives of young people trying to be saved, and it is important to help them fight for their lives and not simply give up on them. So, the U.S. government still has to re-strategize on how to handle the drug war issue because clearly, the old ways are not leading anyone to any progress.

How Much Does the U.S. Government Spend On Border Security

Homeland security

Homeland security is a cabinet department tasked with responsibilities in public security. Its missions basically involve anti-terrorism, border security, immigrations and customs, cyber security and disaster prevention and management. It was created after the September 9/11 attack. Under homeland security lies the U.S. customs and border protection whose sole task is to enforce America's laws along its international borders including the enforcement of immigration laws and policies. The customs and border protection is mainly charged with preventing terrorist and terrorist weapons from entering the states. It is also mandated to apprehend individuals trying to enter America illegally.

In the year 2013, American citizens paid an outstanding $12 billion dollars to facilitate border security actions. The U.S. customs and border protection believes it is important to adequately invest in border security as in turn, it reduces the number of people attempting to enter the country illegally. About 70 percent of the $12 billion is spent on inspections and trade facilitation at or between ports of entry and administration, with 14 percent going to mandatory fees. Is the investment worth the return? Illegal immigration generally affects the security, safety and welfare of the Americans.

Border patrol

Border controls are put in place by a country to impose monitoring or regulation of its borders. The border controls restrict movement of people, goods, and animals into and out of a country. Government agencies are created to help conduct the border controls. Some of the functions performed by such agencies are such as customs, immigration, security, and quarantine, beside other functions. The official jurisdictions, designations, as well as command structures of the agencies will vary considerably from one country to another. However, many may argue that the amount of money spent is too much that it doesn't retaliate back to the economy and it may not be such a good investment.

It is estimated that the amount of American taxpayer's money spent on securing the America–Mexico border between 2000 and 2010 amounted to $90 billion. This amount includes various expenses such as the deployment of National Guard troops to the border, their average salaries, and the cost of procuring machines used to search people at the borders such as surveillance cameras and the likes. There is also the cost of building fences round the Mexican border and also the use of drones to safeguard this border. [85]

With all this money at stake and very reliable manpower at their disposal, the results must be quite outstanding. It was reported that in 2000 about 1.6 million illegal aliens were caught trying to enter the United States of America. In 2010, the number drastically reduced to 463,000 and many attribute this decline to the fact that America has lost its appeal as the dream destination due to rising factors like unemployment and a sluggish economy, just to name a few. Due to this, the number of people worth risking their lives to cross the border have significantly declined and clearly has very little to do with border security efforts. Then comes the question whether all this money spent on border security is really necessary.

Only 44 percent of the U.S.-Mexico border is under operational costs and in an estimate for every one illegal immigrant caught crossing the border, three manage to get through. The money spent on adequately safeguarding the border is all a hoax. It is generally known that nothing can be 100 percent effective and migration has been a matter that has been there for centuries. Is it accurate to say that all these efforts will help stop an age-old phenomenon? All in all, the measures taken are still managing to produce results and that is a huge plus.

FBI

The government has reportedly spent more money on immigration enforcement than all other federal law enforcement agencies when combined. A report by the Migration Policy Institute shows that in the budget for the year 2012, the government had spent an estimated $18 billion on immigration programs. The continued use of too much to enforce immigration policies and reforms shows the weight of the matter. The immigration enforcement seems to be the chief criminal law enforcement priority of the federal government, when judged on the foundation of money allocation it receives and the enforcement actions placed.[86]

The expansive stretch of the U.S. border with Mexico extending nearly 2,000 miles forms a territory that is used by drug cartel groups and their street gang enforcers to ply a perilous and costly trade involving human smuggling, murder, extortion, and corrupt public officials. These are crimes thriving in a multi-billion-dollar industry. They surely pose a threat to communities on living on sides of the border as well as the national security. We however have a problem concerning corrupt border guards. These are guards at the border checkpoint that wave truckloads of whatever— that could be a truckload of narcotics, it could be a truckload of illegal aliens, or it could be pieces of the next dirty bomb that comes into this country. Even if all these measures are put in place, they amount to nothing if the people enforcing these reforms are not on the same team and thus elements such as corrupt officials really slow down the government's operations to safeguard the border.

The FBI's jurisdiction doesn't cover border security but in a bid to adequately secure the border, it has intervened in helping its counterparts in homeland security combat issues like drug trafficking and other drug related crimes.

CIA

The CIA is basically tasked to collect and analyze information from foreign countries on threats to national security. The CIA has no jurisdiction to arrest anyone and basically operates on foreign ground. This is particularly important in securing the border as the CIA helps in acquisition of information about illegal immigration patterns. The CIA, working together with homeland security will definitely help in combating illegal immigration especially with the information from the CIA; this may lead to more arrests and improved security.

From October 2013 through September 2014, US Customs and Border Protection apprehended 68,541 unaccompanied children from Central America and Mexico and 68,445 non-citizens in family units near the US-Mexico border. These figures represent 77 percent and 361 percent increases from the previous year, respectively. Responding to this, the administration of President Obama radically stretched out detention of unauthorized families and ordered for deportations. The Human Rights Watch in October gave a documentation of how migrants from Central America who had escaped to the U.S. in fear that they would be killed were subjected to deportation without giving them sufficient opportunity to seek for protection.

The Obama administration in June is said to have opened the first among three new family detention centers that were supposed to hold and facilitate deportation of children and mothers who had fled Central America. Most of the families that were detained were seeking asylum; surprising, even when the administration discovers that they indeed had fear of getting back to their country, it has failed to release them on bond. The government has categorically argued that these detainees are a "national security" threat, a decision that has been made without duly conducting personal individual risk assessments. The CIA plays a very important role in helping to safeguard the border by its surveillance around the region. With the help of spies on the ground, this will definitely help infiltrate the drug networks and even cartels who control the patterns of illegal migration around this region. This aids in ensuring the citizens of America are properly guarded.

Military

The military is not entitled to secure the borders; the Armed Forces generally provide support to law enforcement and immigration authorities along the Southern border. The reported increase in criminal activity and illegal immigration, however, has alarmed legislators and encouraged them to evaluate the extent and type of military support that occurs in the border region. For instance, in May 25, 2010, President Obama announced that up to 1,200 National Guard troops would be sent to the border to help in supporting border patrols. However, tackling issues of domestic laws and activities pertaining the military, could run opposite to the law of the Posse Comitatus Act (PCA) prohibiting use of the Armed Forces in performing the tasks of civilian law enforcement without explicit authorization.

Other means of legal authorities for deploying the armed forces exist, and the exact scope of permitted activities and funds may vary with the authority being exercised. The National Guard is the branch of the military force that is shared by the states and the federal government, and often assists in counterdrug and counterterrorism efforts.

The term "National Guard" refers to the Army National Guard and the Air National Guard. They are often referred to as the "organized militia", however, when in a federal status, the organization is referred to as the Army National Guard of the United States and the Air National Guard of the United States, and these are the reserve components of the Army and Air Force. They assist border patrol in their activities by basically patrolling the area and also surveillance of the area. They work under the sole authority and control of the president. Though, they are not constitutionally tasked to handle immigrations issues, they can however lend assistance to border security through legislative action.

Infrastructure

Under the administration of President Obama, the resources allocated in the support of the Southwest border by the Department of Homeland Security (DHS) are perceived to be at an all-time high. Currently, about 3,000 more Border Patrol agents have been deployed along the Southwest border, and our unguarded aircraft surveillances, border fencing, and ground surveillances apparatus and systems have almost more than doubled from 2008. Taken as a whole, the additional boots on the ground, technology, and resources provided in the last six years give rise to one of the gravest and unrelenting effort to secure USA's border in history. This has cut illegal border crossings by more than half. By enhancing our infrastructure and technology, the President's proposal continues to strengthen our ability to remove criminals and apprehend and prosecute threats to our national security.

The Border Protection (CBP) has spent an estimate of $385,100,000 on border security, infrastructure, and technology in the year 2012. In the year 2013, it spent about $399,430,000 on border security and infrastructure and technology. In the year 2014, it spent about $351,454,000 on the same provisions. CBP is mandated to secure America's borders from terrorist threats, while at the same time being able to facilitate legitimate trade, travel, and immigration. Such an important role is conducted by CBP's personnel, in addition to use of technology, intelligence, targeting, infrastructure, and a wide range of other capabilities and assets.[87]

CBP also partners with Federal, State, local, tribal, and international stakeholders to perform its mission. Thus, it is very vital for the government to provide the necessary resources and funding needed to carry out these activities. It is also paramount to provide for proper avenues for procuring the devices needed, especially in infrastructure and technology. The improved infrastructure is scheduled to help reduce the number of illegal immigrants crossing the border and also drastically reduce the cases of drug trafficking along the border.

Does stopping Drugs at the Border stop Usage? Or Just increase the Profit of Traffickers

The illegal drug market in the United States is one of the most profitable in the world. The market attracts the most aggressive, ruthless, and sophisticated drug traffickers. It is very challenging for the drug law enforcement agencies to protect the borders of the country. The U.S.-Mexico border is considered the notorious point where much of the cocaine is being smuggled into the U.S.

A recent inter-agency intelligence assessment report, estimates that about 65 percent of the cocaine that is smuggled into the U.S. enters through the Southwest border. It is a substance that's is readily available almost in all major cities in U.S. The worldwide supply of cocaine is controlled by organized crime groups that operate in Colombia. Such organizations use an advanced infrastructure to smuggle cocaine by sea, land, and air into the U.S.

In the U.S., these groups doing their activities from Columbia operate drug money laundering and cocaine distribution networks made up of a huge infrastructure of numerous cells that function in majority of the metropolitan areas. Each cell performs a specific function within the organization such as transportation, local distribution, or money movement. Key managers in Colombia continue to oversee the overall operation.

Less Profits for Cartels?

The increasing number of drug-trafficking organizations (DTOs) within the country of Mexico has ignited increased criminal activities on either side of the border and has dealt a blow to the economy considered a critical trading partner of the U.S. It is estimated that since 2006, close to more than 60,000 people lost their lives in violence related to DTOs while more than 26,000 are said to be missing. In controlling these cartels, it would require that authorities understand the way they function. These are a group of criminal enterprises operating in Mexico as drug-trafficking organizations.

The sale of cocaine, heroin, marijuana, and meth remains extremely profitable. The U.S. Justice Department has put the cartels' U.S. drug trade at $39 billion annually. The border being one of the most protected places, yet the technology and money dedicated to enhancing security there have not been enough to stop this cartels taking. For instance, the Sinaloa Cartel who have extensive underground tunnels that facilitate drug and human trafficking. The cartels have diversity in the range of products that bring them money. This includes human trafficking, sex workers, drugs and other illegal contraband. As the revenue streams of the cartels' become more and more diversified, it's likely that the drug trade may become less and less important. This therefore means that reducing drugs at the border doesn't result in less profit and at most times, these cartels come up with crafty ways to beat the system.

Less Use in the USA

One of the fundamentals of business is that the more profitable markets tend to draw many fresh entrants. Even if the government was to halt the drug supply into the United States of America, it wouldn't lessen the use as these cartels would definitely find a way to manipulate the system. This is because of consumer demand. As long as there is a market among the Americans, the cartels will diligently work to supply products to suite this markets' demand. The cartels, together with corruption and violence, perpetrate and pose threats to Mexico and the U.S. alike. The problem is a complicated one and taps areas of profound policy disagreement. Seeing as to the fact that these cartels have connections everywhere and their drug links are very strong and fully functional, stopping the entrance at the border won't stop their distribution as they will look for alternative means of getting the product to the market. Some will even go as far as catapulting their products into the borders. Most of these cartels have established networks deep-rooted in American soil and this even facilitates easier distribution. Issues like corruption amongst border officials facilitates their distribution and these cartels take advantage of this loophole.[88]

Any measure of Success?

Supply reduction is an essential component of a well-balanced strategic approach to drug control. Demand reduction cannot be successful without limiting drug availability. Thus seizing of drugs at the border at the long run helps control the shipment of drugs. Many may argue that this only increases the net worth of the drugs and doesn't benefit the country, but in a real sense, it limits the drug availability thus limits its use. It is a well thought out fact that a readily available drug would most likely be abused and lead to detriment in the society. Even though the government may put on their best efforts, they will never be able to seize all the drugs entering the United States boundaries.

However, the fewer drugs that arrive at the boundaries the less that arrives in the country. Drug traffickers are flexible, and working on finding a way to beat them would reap good results. The FBI reports record drug arrests of 1.6 million people annually and tons of illegal drugs have been seized, and this is huge step towards the war on drugs.

In the year 2012, the U.S. patrolled 5,000 miles of the Canadian border and 1,900 of the Mexican border, they seized 23,000 violations of intellectual property rights, $1.2 billion in counterfeit goods and 4.2 million pounds of narcotics, and apprehended 365,000 undocumented immigrants. This was a huge burst and one can clearly see the results paying off. The increased efforts towards securing the border and ensuring the safety of American citizens will definitely assist in the war against drugs and help reduce the effect the cartels have in the region.[89]

Is it simple Economics of Supply and Demand?

It is estimated that 45 million U.S. citizens have used an illegal drug. This is just to say that drug dealers have a great market on American soil. Basically, according to the theory of supply and demand, it is described as the state where as supply increases the price will tend to drop or vice versa, and as demand increases the price will tend to increase or vice versa. Now, putting this theory to work, we can see if the government of America decides to cut all avenues of drug trafficking, the supply of drugs will decrease meaning the price will increase. The cartels will be cashing out millions, if not billions, as the value of the drugs increases. In a country where an estimated 45 million citizens have ever tried using an illegal drug the demand is bound to increase. Also in the instance the government cuts off the drug supply, the demand is bound to increase and thus the price will increase and more money for the cartels. In both scenarios, the cartels benefit.

Over the years the prices of cocaine and heroin have reduced, this is to mean that its supply has greatly increased and narcotics users easily access their drugs. The government has a hard task ahead of it as it is clearly losing the war on drugs.

A particularly distinct element of drug trafficking markets is the intermingling of the supply and demand sides. Many people who use illegal drugs also engage in selling the drugs. It should also be noted that frequent users account for a large percentage of the drug selling labor and the sellers account to a large portion of the total consumption of the illegal drugs. Selling of these drugs is a high opportunistic activity and most people who partake in it do so occasionally.

Users of these illegal drugs provide a ready low-wage labor for the illegal market. Thus side measures like expanded treatment will raise distribution costs for drugs as it takes users out of the drug selling ring. For example, in the sale of marijuana, users play an important role as most marijuana users also sell the drug. These markets rely on addiction as it is a very distinctive feature.

How Much Does the Us Spend Fighting Drugs

The U.S. federal government spent over $15 billion dollars in 2010 on the War on Drugs, at a rate of about $500 per second.

In the period spanning the last four decades, over $1 trillion has been used by federal and state governments in fighting the drug war and all that came from the taxpayers who had to foot the bill. Sadly, such huge sums of money and a burden to taxpayers have been a waste considering that distribution and supply of drugs in U.S. continues to be rampant.

In 1980, the United States had 50,000 people behind bars for drug law violations. When we look at these figures now, we have more than half a million people. The U.S. is presently considered to be the largest jailer in the word, and drugs are widely available while treatment resources are shrinking. With more billions of tax dollars having been wasted at the expense of other services, it appears that drug war spending is not yielding any positive results. Important services have been defunded. The huge dollar amount going into drug enforcement means there is less funding going to more serious crimes while at the same time, essential services like health, education, public safety, and social services programs are struggling to run on meager funds. Indeed, all these efforts have not brought out any significant changes in the war against drugs.

How Much is Spent Procuring Drugs

An estimated $100 billion is spent by drug users in the U.S. every year on marijuana, heroin, cocaine, and meth. This total figure may have been stable in the past decade, however, there are compositional shifts that have been witnessed. For example, in 2000, more dollars were spent on cocaine compared to marijuana but in 2010, it was the opposite. This may be attributed to the new legalization of marijuana, which has seen its prices go down. From the year 2002 to 2010, the amount of marijuana consumption in the country went up by close to 30 percent whereas cocaine consumption plummeted by close to 50 percent. Such figures seem to be consistent with indicators of supply-side including seizures as well as estimates on production. What this means is that marijuana was more available in the years something that caused its prices to go down due to forces of demand and supply. Due to its availability, the price of marijuana reduced. For all of the contenders in this drug business to thrive, they basically rely on the total consumption and expenditures driven by the minority of heavy users, who consume for a duration of 21 or more days each month.

Money Spent by US in Patrolling, Arresting, Prosecuting and Maintaining Drug Users in Jail

People arrested in 2014 in the U.S. for violations of drug law were approximately 1,561,231 persons. Of these arrests, about 1,297,384 (83 percent) were believed to be possession only. In the same year, arrests for violation of marijuana laws in the country were 700,993 individuals and among these 619,809 or 88 percent were arrests possession only. Moreover, in 2014, the figure of Americans who were incarcerated in state, federal, as well as local prisons and jails amounts to 2,224,400 or roughly 1 in every 111 American adults.

The percentage of individuals of black or Latino community incarcerated in connection with drug offense among the state prisons was 57 percent, though these groups tend to sell or use drugs at comparable rates to whites. In the period between 1973 and 2014, records of arrests crimes related to drugs were as follows:

In 1973, there were 328,670 arrests that were reported by Uniform Crime Reports (UCR) of the FBI for violating drug law, and this was out of a totaling record of 9,027,700 individuals arrested nationwide for all kinds of offenses. Also that year, authorities reported 380,560 arrests for all violent crime activities and an estimated 1,448,700 arrested individuals for offenses related to property.

In 2014, there were 1,561,231 arrests for drug law violations out of a total 11,205,833 arrests nationwide for all kinds of offenses. Also in 2014, authorities reported 498,666 arrests for all violent crime activities and 1,553,980 arrests for all kinds of property offenses.

The narcotics trade has also significantly impeded growth and stability by diverting limited resources away from more-productive uses. Between the years 1981 and 2008, federal, state, as well as local governments are thought to have spent more than $600 billion (an amount adjusted for inflation) on matters pertaining to drug interdiction and such related law enforcement efforts. When we factor in costs attached to treatment and rehabilitation of addicts, it shoots up to a staggering chunk of money amounting to $800 billion. Not only that, if you were to add what we call 'invisible' losses arising from reduced workplace productivity or curtailed job opportunities, then it implies that the true cost would surely be much higher.

Some may argue that the government is spending a lot of money only to get minimal if no results at all. In the year 2010, the state spent about $48.5 billion on corrections. State spending on corrections basically results in building prisons and the cost it will take to operate the prisons. In the year 2012, the government spent roughly about $53.1 billion on correctional facilities and in 2013 it spent $53.3 billion.

How much Does It spend in Prevention Programs?

In the year 2005 the government set aside $ 8.8 billion for the purposes of prevention, treatment and research and only $ 7.2 billion was dedicated to prevention and treatment. Substance abuse treatment is more cost-effective than prison or other punitive measures. Drug treatment is very beneficial in terms of cost as for every dollar spent on drug treatment, about $18.52 is expected to return to benefit the society. The good thing is that preventive approach is more cost effective or inexpensive, meaning for each dollar spent on the program, it is able to reduce the consumption of cocaine the same way as some enforcement strategies — although it may not be same as the treatment approach or programs. A nationwide school-based prevention program would cost only a tiny fraction of what the U.S. presently spends on drug control, but at this point in the epidemic, its effect on the cocaine-user population would be small and slow to accumulate.

If the government was to revert its focus for a little while, it would realize that the money it has spent on prisons and other drug curbing initiatives was all a waste when they should have in-deed been focusing on how to prevent its influence. Prevention may be a bit too late as already a lot of people are hooked on these drugs and the next alternative should basically be treatment. Treatment is much less costly when compared to its alternatives like incarceration of addicts. For instance, it would cost about $4,700 per patient on average to receive maintenance treatment for methadone in a year. On the contrary, it would cost about $24,000 per person to meet imprisonment costs for a year. This means that government needs to shift its focus by paying more attention to treatment because this is what is going to help the country deal with the menace of drug addiction and probably the issue of drug trafficking.

How many Americans use Illegal Drugs?

It is approximated that around 45 million Americans have ever used an illegal drug. The fact that there is actual demand for illegal drugs is a major setback to the war on drugs. How can you work to eradicate drugs from the country when the people in the country really want those drugs you are trying to get rid of? The following are statistics on substance use in America in the year 2013 carried out by the National Survey On Drug Use and Health where about 67,800 people participated in the survey.

In the year 2013, it was estimated that about 24.6 million Americans between the ages 12 and older had used an illegal drug in the past month. The survey conducted also found out that marijuana was the most commonly abused drugs and other hard drugs like cocaine use stabilized. Cocaine use has recorded a depreciation, as in the year 2013, the number of users aged 12 and older was 1.5 million though lower than in the year 2000 where it was 2 million and 2007 where it was 2.4 million. The use of meth was higher in 2013 with approximately 595,000 users; this was an increase from 353,000 users in the year 2010.[90]

The survey also discovered that most people use drugs for the first time when they are teenagers. In the year 2013, there were just over 2.8 million new users of illegal drugs and over half the number of the new users were under the age of 18. Drug use was recorded highest among people between their late teens and their twenties. Drug use is also increasing among people in their fifties and their sixties. It is important for the government to work to reduce these numbers in order to effectively partake on the war on drugs. It would be difficult to work with these high numbers if they really want to curb drug and substance abuse.

How much Does the US spend in Preventing Drugs from Coming in?

The government spends a lot of money on preventing drugs from coming into the country. In the year 2013, the department of defense pledged to support federal, state, and local drug law enforcement agencies requests for domestic operational costs. The government set aside $146.9 million for the sake of improved security along the border. It cost about $100 billion every year to enforce the drug control system. Federal spending in the U.S. alone accounts to a totals of close to $15 billion in a year and one estimate indicated that the local and state drug-related crime justice expenditures clocked $25.7 billion. Much of the allocated money goes towards procuring of advanced equipment's to help in detection or in purchasing drones to help in surveillance missions. The allocated funds may also be used to pay and also increase the number of people working at the borders.

Given the current economic conditions, it is more important than ever that spending is effective and not a waste of tax-payers money. The huge investments in enforcement have consistently delivered the opposite expected results to reduce drug production and supply and instead, they have created a more lucrative business. It may be said that, there exists a big opportunity cost in relation to wasted expenditure on this level when you consider that drug enforcement budget is inflating and continues to grow while other areas remain starved of funds. The reduction in budget is hard hitting things like public services and the support for people needing assistance. This in something that brings about economic and social costs through criminal activities and poor health outweighing the billions being spent on enforcement.

What is the Total US Drug Usage Cost?

The economic cost of drug abuse in the U.S. was projected at $193 billion in the year 2007, which is the last available estimate. This value includes:

- About $120 billion that went to loss in productivity, because of costs related to labor participation, drug abuse participation, incarceration, as well as premature death.
- Close to $11 billion that went to healthcare costs – for drug addiction treatment as well as other medical consequences related to drugs use
- Another $61 billion that went to criminal justice costs, basically due to prosecution, criminal investigation, incarceration, and victim costs.[91]

There is an alarming number of people involving themselves in drug abuse and this issue needs to be adequately addressed. The labor force is affected very much by the increased use of drugs and this in turn leads to absenteeism, poor performance in school, truancy just to mention a few. Millions of dollars are spent trying to acquire drugs that will in turn endanger one's life or just be a detriment to the society instead of putting the money to aid in public development or enhancement of the community. It is really alarming that the number of people using illicit drugs is increasing. This means the cartels get really good money and is a major setback to the war on drugs.

It is about time the government went back to the drawing board and came up with an efficient way to curb drug influence in the country. It is appreciated that the government is making efforts to really tackle this, but the drug traffickers seem to be way ahead of them and are easily finding a way to manipulate their efforts. It should be noted that more emphasis should be placed on prevention and treatment than on prison facilities, as this will save more money. All in all, the sale of illicit drugs will always be there as long as there is a market or demand for the drugs and finding a way to quash the demand will be the much needed breakthrough in this struggle.

The Illegal Issue

Why do people from Latin America immigrate without documentation to the USA?

In an interview with sociologist Dr. Erika Arenas, an Associate Professor at University of California, Santa Barbara, visiting scholar at The California Center for Population Research at UCLA and Mexican immigration expert, it appears that the reason for people immigrating illegally has changed over the years.

The term illegals, undocumented, aliens, violent, and other labels have been used in different scenarios to portray different meanings for Mexicans in the USA. It is a game applied by politicians to gain their motives. In the old days, when American needed workers to work in the construction, farming, and other sectors, it allowed Mexicans to come in fast. The whole idea of labeling Mexicans living in America as illegals is unfounded. The Mexicans who came to the United States to work because they were needed here, are now being said to have come illegally. They are now being called illegal immigrants.

Illegal is the term used when someone violates the law, such as in the case of murder. It is a powerful term used by politicians to spread fear and prejudice in return for votes.

The power of this word is almost unrivaled in the emotion it creates and the harm it spreads.

The word Illegal could also be used for someone speeding on the freeway. Anyone who ever broke the speed limit law is an illegal. Yes, this statement is true, however the word illegal just lost a bit of power. In California driving at 66 miles per hour on the five freeway would make you an illegal. On the other side of the argument, the term undocumented worker does not stir images of people coming to do harm. It portrays images of people working. This does not encourage hate, plant ideas of people breaking the law, and will not get any votes. So politicians will continue to use dividing language for votes until they are forced by the voters to change.

One major part of the interview with Dr. Arenas focused on Immigration trends of Mexicans to U.S. Dr. Arenas says that there are programs like the Bracero program and others where temporary visas are given to people who want to work in USA. People come to the U.S. work, make money and they go back home. They do not have to stay because they are not interested in staying. This is one form of immigration and it's seasonal, but then there is another type of immigration which isn't seasonal. It involves people who have no opportunities in Mexico. There are people tired of being in Mexico and want to seek opportunities in the USA. These people have social connections meaning they know people who are in the U.S. So, they need to have money or save to come to the USA. The poorest people cannot come to the U.S. because they don't have the money and the more time elapses, the more difficult it becomes because it is getting expensive to come to the country. There are the 'coyotes' who help them cross to the U.S. but they charge more.

According to Dr. Arenas, there is a populous believe that the poorest economic class of Mexico is the one immigrating to the USA. "This is simply incorrect" she says. Immigrating to the US is expensive. Especially if you earn a minimum wage of $30 per week. It would take years to save up for a trip to the USA.

An individual needs about $1000 to $3000 depending on where they live in Mexico to get crossed to the U.S. This does not include traveling costs. Many immigrants come with passports and simply stay in the country.

Immigrants from Mexico usually have a relative, friend, or someone they know and most likely they already have a job when they enter the USA. In some cases, if they don't have the money, they're financed by people already in the U.S. to help them cross over. The same people secure jobs for their friends and relatives once they cross the border. This is a very important economic and immigration trend. Immigrants coming from Mexico have jobs even before they get into the country. This is a tremendous encouragement for immigrants. It also makes them taxpayers and contributors to the US economy from day one. This immigration is territorial. One group from a Mexican town goes to another town in the USA. For example, people coming from Yucatan and especially the 'Muna' area, go to the city of Oxnard in California and work at restaurants. They can work in the kitchen and other areas. It is this social structure and connection that allows migration to become more fluid.

Many Mexicans who immigrated to the U.S. in the past have returned home. Many intended to do so from the beginning, others miss their families and way of life, others get sick and have to return. There're those who come to the US, work, save money and go back to Mexico.

In the 2008 recession, a lot of people who had crossed to the U.S. returned because they were laid off from the construction jobs. Many others came to the U.S. and didn't like the way of life, so they left the country and returned home. Many Anglo-Americans cannot believe that a Mexican would come to the country and return home. It is shocking for them to hear that a Mexican immigrant can come and dislike the place. Situations where immigrants return to Mexico are a common thing, but theories have always depicted that all immigrants come and stay.

There is a perception among Anglo-Americans that people come to America because it is the greatest country in the world. However, what they don't realize is that Mexicans come to America to work and when they get money, they go back home because Mexico for them is the greatest country in the world.

There are Americans who go to Mexico and live there because it is a beautiful country. It's a great place to live— the weather is beautiful. Alejandro Portes has written a book titled *The Immigrant America* and it brings out theories based on reception of immigrants here in Mexico. They will choose if they stay or they do not.

So, it can be seen that when people go to a place where they don't get medical services or they have troubles because they speak Spanish, or if they cannot find jobs, they will say they better return based on the context of reception of people. That may be right!

On the other hand, you come to a place and find that you know some of the people there. There are people waiting for you and you get a job the moment you arrive. You also find that there are many people who speak Spanish, and the community is ready to help you because there is your aunt, cousin, close friend, or another relative— certainly based on the theory of reception of people, you will say that "I better stay!"

There are many factors that will determine if someone crossing over from Mexico to U.S. will stay or not. For instance, it is not same for a person who gets to Los Angeles and another who goes to Wisconsin from Mexico.

In Mexico, there is a policy called 'popular insurance' that was launched in 2002 and it has spread all over, and by 2012/13, it almost reached countrywide coverage. This is to mean that every Mexican has health insurance. So, Mexicans who come to the U.S. and find that they cannot have access to medical service because they don't have insurance may decide to go back to Mexico where they get medical attention. Let's say, if they are diagnosed with cancer, they can get medication in Mexico from the 'popular insurance' policy.

Here in the U.S. the undocumented immigrants or Mexicans do not have insurance, not even Obama's program helps them. According to Dr. Arenas' research, there is a correlation between determination of health and the return to Mexico.

Even if the people crossing to U.S. have insurance coverage, some would still return but maybe many would stay. There are people who have crossed to the U.S. and found jobs in construction work. But when these jobs end, they go back to Mexico. Others are injured in those jobs and because they are not insured, they will get back to Mexico to seek medical attention. There are many hypotheses as to why Mexicans are staying and others are returning back home. Perhaps it is something that needs to be explored further with a backup of data. Perhaps what presidential candidates like Trump could say is, "Well, we don't have to give them anything. And as a matter of fact, Mexicans in America are deporting themselves." It's like an auto deportation though it has a price. "As far as Mexican migration trends and movements, the main topic of my research, I've found that many Mexicans move back to Mexico" said Dr. Arenas.

There are theories that hold that once a Mexican gets to the U.S., they never look back to return to their land. However, this is a misconception because many have and many are returning. The reasons for them returning is something that needs to be studied further. It may be because they lose jobs in areas like the construction and with no one to support them, they have to leave for home. It may also be because they have deep roots to their Mexican land and they feel that they want to get back to their roots.

It requires some personality to leave your country, and unless there is war, it is difficult to leave your family, friends, and relatives and decide not to come back. The mental strength of a person can determine if they can stay without having to connect with their family back in Mexico. Even those who legally cross to the U.S., many do return to Mexico.

Who Invented the Term Illegal Aliens?

Following the recent presidential campaigns in the United States of America, there has been a lot of talk of the term illegal aliens popularly quoted by Republicans like Donald Trump. In most of the instances, they refer to the rising numbers of Latin Americans entering American soil illegally. This particular issue is very sensitive as it goes back to even the dawn of the Republic. In a real sense, America has always had immigrants as it was founded by people whose ancestors were not born in America. Therefore, it is very racist to brand a particular group of people illegal aliens.

The quest for a better life has always been an every-day necessity, dating back even to the nineteenth century where the slaves for the slave states were tasked to cross the Mason-Dixon line in order to get to the free states. The Mason-Dixon Line was the national divide between free states and slave states. The Mason-Dixon Line represented a way to attain freedom for thousands of blacks seeking to escape slavery in the south. The line provided a safe haven for many black slaves as it offered hope for a better life with no undue influence or duress.

In the present day situation, the American border provides the much needed hope for a better life with many Latinos willing to risk their lives to attain the American dream. The common means of crossing the border is by hiring people smugglers and they are to help facilitate a means to enter the country. Common reasons for seeking to enter the country illegally include employment, personal and family betterment or seeking to escape unrest. Most people often resort to this method since they are unable to acquire visas or green-cards. This raises the question whether the quest for a better life is wrong.

In recent years, the number of illegal immigrants has stabilized unlike the past years where there was a great influx of immigrants. Executive actions on illegal immigrants have a long history and the most significant include; the law that was passed in 1986 that allowed 2.7 million unauthorized immigrants to obtain green cards and the most recent being President Obama's executive action that would expand deportation relief to almost half the unauthorized immigrant population. This decision however has been hotly contested by the Republicans who are of contrary opinion.

What Motivates a Person to Leave his/her Country?

The United States of America is viewed as an extremely desirable destination. Depending on the region you are coming from, most come to the country for a variety of reasons like personal betterment, economic reasons, or to escape political oppression. The most popular motivation for people to leave their countries for the United States of America is due to economic reasons. Most illegal immigrants who get jobs in America are paid higher than they would be in their very own countries. Illegal immigrants are able to get jobs due to the following reasons; global economic change, inadequacy of channels for legal economic migration and ineffective employer sanction. Global economic change has fostered their economies to invest with outsiders thus increasing the number of low-skilled workers. This has killed the number of low- income workers in Mexico and increased the demand of low-income workers in America thus it is very logical that Mexicans cross the borders to seek employment opportunities, which they lack in their native countries. The ineffectiveness of current employer sanctions for illegal hiring allows immigrants to easily find jobs. Take for instance, it is unlawful to hire an illegal immigrant knowingly but the means and methods of detection are very uncertain thus a huge loophole in this particular law.

The Bracero program facilitated the immigration of Mexicans to work temporarily in farm jobs. The Americans at that time needed labor and relied on their southern counterparts to help provide labor. The program encouraged circular migration patterns that continued even after the program ended. This program ran from 1942-1964 and its main aim was to have Mexicans in the country as guest workers. Almost all of the legal temporary workers became illegal immigrants when they chose to still work in America even after the program was terminated. This program was faulted for facilitating a large number of Mexicans to enter the country illegally while they did not have the set qualifications to work as guest workers in the country. Most of these guest workers' main aim was actually to just earn money and send it to their families back at their native land. They are basically driven by their commitment to provide their families with economic security. The gap between third-world countries and first-world countries increases yearly and thus people move to more stable economies to earn a better living and basically to escape poverty.

The decision to migrate to America illegally is not only induced by economic prosperity. It takes a lot of thinking through to leave everything behind and go to a new land for betterment. Many make the decision after considering a lot of things, one of them includes if any family or friends have successfully crossed the border. It's is quite a dangerous affair and one may stand to risk arrest but looking at the benefits that come with the American dream, many go for the risk. It should be noted that most people would not consider going to a foreign land if they did not know anyone there and this is a fact many people consider before attempting to enter America illegally.

How Many Undocumented Workers Right Now?

According to Pew Research Center, there were about 11.3 million unauthorized immigrants. Their population has stabilized for the past five years. The actual number of undocumented immigrants is difficult to tell due to the fact that facilitating the means to count the people in this category is hard, so most findings are estimates.

Illegal Aliens in the Past

The Pew Hispanic Center estimates that the basic number of undocumented immigrants entering America in the 1980's was around 130,000 per year. It increased to 450,000 between the years 1990-1994 and greatly increased to 750,000 in the period of 1995-1999. Since 2000, the influx has increased to more than 500,000 undocumented immigrants per year. The noticeably highest influx in the number of undocumented immigrants was noted in 2007, as their number increased to a surprising 12.2 million.

How Many "Illegal Aliens" are now Legal?

The number of illegal aliens who have attained legal status is vague. However, there is good news for many illegal immigrants as President Obama moves to give legal status to five million immigrants. Though this decision is hotly contested, it seeks to help many illegal immigrants to attain citizenship status.

Breaking the Law: It's Not Always Black and White, or Bronze and White!

A great argument against immigration is that you should not break the law. This writer has personally experienced this application of the law. Many laws are created to win campaigns. Calling people illegals might stir a certain voting community, creating a law against these illegals could make the same politician get reelected without any regard to the law's social, economic, or humanitarian implications. Such are the immigration laws of the USA.

What if the law was established after breaking more, larger, international laws? This is the case of the greatest land expansion of US territory. Land acquired illegally, then applying laws to protect it.

You Are Now Illegal. How The U.S. Stole Mexico

The Annexation of Texas, the Mexican-American War, and the Treaty of Guadalupe-Hidalgo, 1845–1848

The U.S. invaded Mexico with malice aforethought. The reason? Declare war and take over land. The new acquired territory was to expand the power of southern states in economic and political value. This would ensure a majority of southerners in congress and the protection of savers. The act was done with malice, and the reasons for doing it villainous.

U.S. President James K. Polk was in power at the time of the Mexican-American War that was fought from 1846 to

1848. This is presumably the first armed conflict for the U.S. to fight outside of its soil. The aim was to expand the territory of the United States of America to the Pacific Ocean. By the time the dust cleared, Mexico found itself without close to a third of its territory, which includes the present day Utah, Arizona, Nevada, California, and New Mexico.

Apparently, just days before Mexico could cede the land to U.S. in the Guadalupe Hidalgo Treaty, gold had been discovered in California.

The events of the Mexican-American War brought within the control of the United States the future states of Texas, California, Nevada, New Mexico, Arizona, Utah, Washington, and Oregon, as well as portions of what would later become Oklahoma, Colorado, Kansas, Wyoming, and Montana.

Expansion with War or Theft?

The states of New Mexico and other portions of the southwest region are internationally recognized as provinces in Mexico. This was before America waged war on Mexico and took these states from them. So, in a real sense, the Mexicans fleeing their country to states like New Mexico are not exactly illegal. A historic injustice that happened in the past has shaped their lives to think they are illegally placed while in reality they are the original occupants of that particular land and deserve to be there by right.

This all dates back to 1844 when James Polk was campaigning to be President and expressed his wish to expand America's territory to Mexico. During his inauguration he confided in his Secretary of the Navy that his main objective as President was to acquire California, which Mexico was refusing to sell. President Polk promised Texas that he would move the Texas-Mexico border. He then ordered troops to march into Mexican inhabited territory causing them to flee and clearly inciting provocation.

Polk was responsible for incitement of war on this region, which was hotly disputed. The Americans were easily able to defeat the Mexicans with ease, but was it justified? They clearly used their status to oppress a struggling nation. Waging a war for no apparent reason just to grab territory was illegal under international law, and to this day unjust. The US marched on Iraq for the very same reason on the first Iraq war. Siting injustice and the protection of the sovereign country of Kuwait.

Many have battled on what to call it, with the Mexicans referring to it as the U.S. invasion and the Americans referring to it as the Mexican war. It was quite clear that America violated the 1828 border treaty that recognized Mexico's sovereignty over the region. To add insult to injury, America was just taking Texas from Mexico's jurisdiction. It should have been a warning signal to Mexico that other regions close to Texas were also of interest to the Americans. President Polk's decision to invade Mexico had raised so many flags. Was it truly a means of protecting the United States of America borders or an invasion into Mexican soil?

The war had officially begun to a very unfortunate nation with a powerful enemy seeking to forcefully acquire their territory. Plainly speaking a war was never declared on America but the need to defend its territory necessitated a fight. It is safe to say that America's aggression caused the war that was obviously very unjust.

The Invisible Hand

Supply and demand is one of the basis of American folklore, economy and mythology. Supply and Demand, the best entrepreneur or employee wins the job or the contract. Except if you're willing to work cheaper and do it better. Then we'll stop you from coming in because we don't need that type of competition. This seems to me anti-capitalistic. Forget that many immigrants take on jobs nobody wants. Even if they took on other jobs, isn't the role of Capitalism to give the job to the best candidate? Isn't that best for the consumer?

High Born Royalty

The idea of giving rights depending on your birth status is not something new. It dates back to leaders proclaiming they are the chosen of god, in some cases, the reincarnation of god. We saw it with the Egyptians, with Christian kings of the middle ages, and we see it in modern politics. If you are born of a certain color, or in a certain economic class, you can do more, get more, not go to jail. If you are born on the other side of a fence, under the same universal rights, the same global human rights, even the same rights under church and ethical rights, you are not welcome. This is a very powerful message.

DACA and DAPA

What is DACA and DAPA? Deferred Action for Children Arrivals and Deferred Action for Parents of American citizens are two immigration programs for undocumented residents. DACA are children brought into this country as minors. Sometimes as babies. Many never knew their home country and don't even speak the language of the country where they were born. They are now in the USA with no legal resident status. DAPA are undocumented immigrants who had children in the USA. Those children are US citizens but the parents are not. If those parents are deported, and many have been, they leave their children without parents.

In my interview with Lizet Ocampo of *the Center* for *American Progress Action Fund* I found out how important these programs are for immigrants and for the country. Not to mention the social implications of not deporting the parents of US citizens, or immigrants who arrived as children to this country and know no other country. The economic implications are also immense as we'll see in the next paragraphs. Lizet Ocampo provided much of the research on DACA and DAPA used in the book.

DACA and DAPA provide a solutions for immigrants to stay in the country without the nightmarish fear of deportation, but they're far from a good solution for the immigrants and for the country according to Athenea Luciano, author of US Immigration Ultimate Guide and former Homeland Security Officer. "It's like lifetime probation" she told me in an interview. "They are not even second class citizens, not even bastard children" she said. Athenea is passionate about immigration. Her father was deported as a child, even though she was a US citizen. "The process is egalitarian," she said. I'm sitting in her office in San Diego, California. I see a badge on her desk framed and behind glass. "My old badge" she said. "We called working on the border blood money" she told me. "Deporting people that are here to work". Speaking about her father still makes her eyes water. She felt hopeless as a child. "If you have money you're in, if you don't, you struggle" she said.

America misses out on immense economic growth each day it fails to address the country's broken immigration system. It is commendable that they put in place the deferred action programs that are an important stepping stone toward a long term solution and will produce economic gains. However, these gains are bound to be overshadowed by the benefits America will gain from having a legislative reform that includes a pathway to citizenship. On comparing the ten-year potential economic impact of no executive action, deferred action and providing a pathway to citizenship to various topics, the outcome resulted into;

- The number of people granted work permits through no executive orders as zero,
- The number of people granted work permits through deferred action at 3.7 million, and-
- The number of people granted work permits through pathway to citizenship at 8 million.

A pathway to citizenship will involve granting legal status to undocumented immigrants and they would then obtain citizenship after five years.

On calculating the increase in gross domestic product (G.D.P), it is noted that there is no cumulative when there is no executive order, but there is a $230 billion increase when there is a deferred action and a $ 1.2 trillion cumulative increase in the G.D.P when there is a pathway to citizenship. It should be further noted that there is also an increase in all Americans income if they allow for the provisions of deferred action and pathway to citizenship. Their cumulative increase in their incomes increase by $124 billion if there is deferred action and $625 billion when there is a pathway to citizenship.

Contrary to popular belief, the American citizens stand to benefit if the immigrants are given legal status. The undocumented immigrants also stand a chance to benefit if they put into place deferred action and pathway to citizenship as they will record a cumulative increase in their income for example, in the place of deferred action, there is cumulative increase of $103 billion and in the instance of pathway to citizenship, there is a cumulative increase of $521 billion.

The number of new jobs created annually will also have a drastic increase with about 29,000 jobs created due to deferred action and about 145,000 jobs created due to pathway to citizenship.

Economic Impacts of Deferred Action via DACA and DAPA

The Deferred Action for Children Arrivals is a policy allowing certain illegal immigrants who come into the nation before they reached their 16th birthday to have a renewable two-year work permit while being exempted from deportation. The Deferred Action for Parents of American citizens and lawful permanent residents is a policy that facilitates the provision of temporary reprieve from deportation and the ability to work lawfully for a temporary period of time to eligible undocumented immigrants.

America stands to benefit immensely through these programs. If the majority of these illegal immigrants attain legal status, it will enable them to search for better jobs that match their skills without the fear of deportation and will be more productive and that is a plus to the economy. Their legal authorization will make them less vulnerable to wage theft and will reduce workplace exploitation thus enhancing job security for this particular group of people. This in turn will lead to higher wages that generate to more tax revenue collected and increased economic activity across the nation.

Granting Deferred Action to undocumented immigrants will result in a number of gains that include an increase in the number of jobs created in the next five years to 21,433 annually and 28,814 jobs created annually in the period of a decade. America's gross domestic product will increase by $86 billion over the period of five years and by $230 billion over the period of ten years. The increasing economy will also facilitate a rise in all Americans income by $46 billion in the period of over five years and by $124 billion over the period of ten years. Beneficiaries of the DACA and the DAPA program will also experience an increase in their incomes by $38 billion over the period of five years and $103 billion over the period of ten years. There indeed is much to gain with the adoption of these policies and the Congress should be looking for ways to enact the policies for the betterment of America's economy and not spending time fighting it. They should thus pay much consideration to the pros of these policies as they stand to benefit all Americans.

Though these policies have sparked a lot of debate, they stand to benefit a lot of families. It is estimated that more than 6.1 million American citizens live with a family who will be in constant fear of deportation if the Supreme Court rules against DAPA. It is projected that the numbers are higher as a lot of other factors were not taken into consideration like U.S. citizen family members of people eligible for DACA or expanded DACA or U.S. citizen children or other family members who do not live in the same household as a DAPA-eligible individual. By putting into action these policies, it will relieve many families from constant worry of deportation of their family members.

Economic Impact of Undocumented Workers

Are Undocumented Immigrants a Burden to the Economy?

Undocumented immigrant workers cannot access public benefits like food stamps, medi-cards or welfare provision as most of these provisions require proof of legal immigration status. It is also quite unfortunate that even legal immigrants cannot receive these benefits unless they have stayed for a period of five years in the country. Children of undocumented immigrants who are citizens of the United States of America get to enjoy these services.

Most notably, the undocumented immigrants have a big role to play in contributing to the nation's economy. It is well known that there are net gains when there is a large labor supply. The unauthorized immigrants form part of a supple workforce, often providing a safety valve during the times when demand seems pressing. The same people are among the first to be sent away when the economy dwindles. It should be emphasized that undocumented immigrants contribute to the economy through their investments and consumption of goods and services; they fill in millions of crucial working positions thereby resulting in what is called subsidiary job creation as well as increased productivity while also being able to lower the costs of services and goods. They also participate in unreciprocated contributions towards social security, unemployment insurance programs, and Medicare.

The total goods and services that they consume through the money they earn, and all that they produce for their employers result to roughly about $800 billion. These undocumented workers typically earn less than if they were legalized. This leads to lower wages and higher profits for the employers. At the same time, it creates a tax surplus for the government, as these workers pay taxes with taxpayer identifications or counterfeit social security numbers but don't collect tax or social security benefits. Not to mention their contribution to the economy as a consumer base.

The US government along with business owners reap the benefits of undocumented immigrants immediately. And we could make the case that the population reaps benefits once the money is used in infrastructure and other benefits. The migrants are treated as second class residents of the country. They pay taxes and social security without collecting it, they can't vote, don't have access to the many of the social benefits they fund with tax dollars; making less money in the process.

Contribution in Taxes, Social Security and the Economy

Undocumented immigrants are paying billions of dollars in taxes to the country and it is estimated to increase if the proposed legislation of protecting these undocumented workers from deportation was to go through. According to an analysis of 50 states done by the Institute On Taxation and Economic Policy, it was estimated that roughly 8.1 million of 11.4 million undocumented immigrants paid more than $11.8 billion in state and local taxes in the year 2012. These estimates are bound to increase by $834 million under the full implementation of Obama's 2012 and 2014 executive actions and by an outstanding 2.2 billion under immigration reform. The analysis shows that undocumented immigrants already pay billions in taxes and are a well needed resource to the American economy and their contribution would be even more fulfilling if they were to legalize their status.

Illegal immigrants not only benefit the nation by providing it with a ready labor force, but also with tax dollars.

Contrary to popular belief, undocumented immigrants pay billions in taxes every year. A report compiled by the non-partisan Congressional Budget Office (CBO) estimated the impact of the immigration bill to generate more than $450 billion in additional federal revenue over the next decade. Just like ordinary people living in America, undocumented immigrants contribute most parts of their income to state and local taxes. In addition to paying sales and excise taxes when they purchase goods and services like utilities, clothing and gasoline, they also pay property taxes on their homes and at least half of them are paying income taxes despite their illegal status.

Undocumented immigrants make up five percent of the labor force and are a small share of most states' population. While it may seem that the aggregate state and local taxes paid to undocumented immigrants in each state seem modest compared to overall tax collections, their effective rate is close to taxpayers in similar income situations and in many states, it can be higher than the effective tax rates paid by upper income taxpayers. The effective rate is the share of tax payer's money that goes to paying taxes. However, these illegal aliens pay billions in taxes on benefits they are often unable to receive.

Unauthorized immigrants pay up to $13 billion a year in social security taxes of which they get back only $1 billion. According to social security administration, they estimated that about 7 million people are working in America illegally and among these about 3.1 million are using fake or expired social security numbers and yet also they pay automatic payroll taxes. This basically amounts to an annual net contribution of $12 billion to the social security trust fund. The SSA also estimates that illegal immigrants have paid an outstanding $100 billion to the fund for the past decade. Unfortunately, due to the fact that they are in the country illegally, it is very unlikely that they will benefit from their contributions to the fund. The earnings of unauthorized immigrants result in a net positive effect in social security financial status and this effect contributes roughly $12 billion to the cash flow of the program.

When there is no verifiable number allowing for payroll contributions to be credited, they are channeled to the Earnings Suspense File. A study that was conducted by the Center of American Progress (CAP) found out that this file is estimated to have accumulated one trillion worth of tax contributions. This is because undocumented workers are paying into the system most of the times with false social security numbers, which means they will never collect their benefits. It is thus safe to say that unauthorized immigrants contribute positively to the financing of social security not only in terms of their contributions but in the succeeding generations when they have children who are American citizens by birth.

Undocumented immigrants have immense importance to America's labor force and if they were to be completely deported, America stands to lose a lot especially since they serve a part of the American economy where most Americans are not willing to work and the number of them working in sectors such as farming and fishing are quite few. They basically boost the economy as most of them go for minimum wage jobs and in most cases minimum wage usually depreciates and thus an increase in income for the average American citizen.

What is the Economic Impact of Legalizing Them?

The proposed legislation of legalizing illegal immigrants has been a very contentious issue and many may beg to differ but it is important to understand that doing so is not only a humanitarian act but also an economic stimulus to America. Workers with legal status earn more than those who work illegally and legalizing them will increase their wages which in turn increases the tax collected and consumer spending which generates jobs. The economic value of the proposed legislation is estimated to amount to tens of billions of dollars in added income, billions of dollars in additional tax revenue and hundreds of thousands of jobs for American citizens and the immigrants as well. Legalization of the otherwise law abiding undocumented immigrants is humane for them and their families and this helps develop a better workforce. Legalization is also bound to level the playing field and create fair competition among American workers which in turn improves the earning of companies and increases the tax revenue of both federal and state governments.

Legal status and citizenship enable illegal immigrants to produce and earn significantly more than they do when they are on the economic sidelines. The resulting productivity and wage gains benefit the economy as they are not only workers but also consumers and tax payers. They are bound to spend their increased earnings on basic necessities like clothing, food, and shelter and this in turn stimulates demand in the economy for jobs and services and thus leads to the creation of more jobs. However, undocumented immigrants are earning far less than their potential, paying less in taxes and contributing significantly less to the economy than they would if they were to obtain legal status which clearly is a benefit to everyone.

There are several reasons why legalization and citizenship both raise the incomes of immigrants and improve economic outcomes. Providing an avenue to attain citizenship for unauthorized immigrants gives them legal protection that raises their wages, something which they do not get to experience when they are working illegally. They get to benefit from the numerous employment rights due to their new legalized status.

Providing these workers with legal status increases their bargaining power relative to their employers which leads to lower likelihood of worker exploitation and guarantees job security. It also promotes in the investment of education and training which will further help them to climb the career ladder and progress to better paying jobs and in the end run increase in the tax revenue collected and also improves the efficiency of the labor market. It also facilitates undocumented immigrants with entrepreneurship benefits like providing access to licenses, permits, insurance and credit to start businesses and create jobs. Immigration reform that promotes the creative potential of immigrant entrepreneurs works to promote economic growth, higher incomes and more job opportunities.

What is the Loss If they are not Documented?

There would be a wide gap in the labor division. Since most immigrants are eager to take up jobs most Americans are not like cleaning houses and farming, it allows for more people to afford cheaper food and better services and thus enabling people to attain more wealth. The economy also stands to lose billions of dollars that would have come in the form of taxes to both state and local government. This is because though they are undocumented most of them pay taxes using fake social security numbers and also from consumer spending, and thus the economy will suffer a dear loss. These immigrants pay up to $11 billion to social security and in most instances they cannot access these benefits which amounts to a great amount of money generated to social security.

Immigrants provide a major source of revenue through their various undertakings. Just by buying goods, this is a substantial loss. They provide a ready labor force for America's economy and this improves the efficiency of the labor market and the economy stands to lose quite a lot if they decide to reject the legalization legislation. According to a survey done in 2010 by the American immigration council and American progress it was realized that deporting all unauthorized immigrants would reduce the country's GDP by 1.46 annually or over $2.6 trillion in lost GDP over 10 years. This would mean a continuous steady drop in the country's GDP. Their contribution to the economy of America is indeed large and cutting this source of economic aid will be a devastating loss to the economy of America.

Though many argue that these unauthorized workers take jobs that were initially meant for American citizens, it is actually quite a deceiving notion as these workers create supply demand and this in turn increases the number of job opportunities in the market. Their contribution to the economy as small business owners will also diminish as they will lose all their benefits and licenses and all the income they put to federal and state tax will not benefit the economy any more. It is quite clear that billions if not trillions of dollars will be lost if America were to decide to deport all unauthorized immigrants and this in turn will hurt the economy by reducing the amount of tax collected, reducing the number of jobs created and creating a large disparity in the labor sector.

The High Economic Cost of Delaying DAPA and Expanded DACA

The current immigration reform brought to light by president Obama was formulated to basically unlock the untapped potential of over 4 million unauthorized immigrants living in America. This reform included the expansion of the Deferred Action for Children Arrivals and the creation of the Deferred Action for Parents of Americans and lawful permanent residents. It is formulated to provide work permits and temporary relief from deportation. If the expanded DACA and the DAPA were to be fully implemented, America's economy would stand to experience immense gains. It is however unfortunate that these policies are not being implemented and the economy loses millions of dollars in gross domestic product each day, and this also means that America loses a great amount of potential economic growth each year. This basically amounts to about $29.9 million U.S. GDP lost every day according to the center of American Progress.

A continuous delay in providing legal status to these workers means that they are in constant worry of being deported. The economy also stands to lose billions of dollars if they are to continue delaying the affirmative action as these workers stand to get a better chance of increased wages if they are legalized, and this in turn will lead to more tax revenue being collected. Providing them will legalization will also offer them job security and a very contented labor force, service delivery will be up to standard, and this in turn will lead to cheaper services. Legalization will also provide the immigrants with the chance to venture into business by helping them acquire licenses and insurances that will help them set up these businesses. This also will create more job opportunities and something that benefits the economy. By delaying on legalizing these undocumented immigrants, the government is basically throwing away all these revenue sourcing businesses. Estimates show that temporary work permits will increase the income of unauthorized immigrants by 8.5 percent by preventing workplace exploitation and finding jobs that best fit their skills.

The council of economic advisers (CEA) estimates that these policies will increase the national gross domestic product by nearly $60 billion in the next decade. This is quite a huge amount of money for the government to choose to miss out by delaying the implementation of the immigrant legalization processes. Local economies also stand to reap benefits from these policies; this is because of the eligibility criteria set for the beneficiaries of the immigration directives. These reforms are sure to source eligible immigrants who will most certainly help improve the economy of America. A study in North Carolina shows that for every one to two immigrant agricultural workers, one new American job is created. This goes to prove that these policies are helping in creating job opportunities and we are losing so many jobs for Americans by delaying the implementation of these immigration reforms. Undocumented immigrants provide more benefits other than the extra tax revenue realized. It is quite a loss stalling these reforms as millions of dollars are just going down the drain.

Prejudice and Racism: How far is too far?

"The less justified a man is in claiming excellence for his own self, the more ready is he to claim excellence for his nation, his religion, his race or his holy cause."
--Eric Hoffer, author of True Believer

Eric Hoffer, the author of the book True Believer, believes that true followers of a mass political movement are the frustrated. "People who feel that their lives are spoiled or wasted," he says. We've seen it throughout history with Nazism as the most famous end extreme example; we see it today with Trump true believers and it resonates with the blame culture. "Our jobs go to Mexico; Jobs are taken by Mexicans."

In this book, Hoffer tries to explain various types of personalities that give rise to mass movements; why and how mass movements start and the similarities between them. He basically argues that even if their ideologies differ, they are interchangeable and this means that the motives for mass movements are also interchangeable.

Hoffer states that mass movements are established by the desire for change rooting from dissatisfied people who have lost complete trust in customs and traditions. They are of the belief that there is no satisfaction in their lives and mask themselves in large masses to gain purpose. Leaders are a very important piece in mass movements but for them to have full success, the fundamental core values of mass movements must be in people's hearts. It should also be noted that all movements have similar elements like the fact that they are all competitive and that they are all interchangeable. Some of the groups who are most likely to be easily convertible are for instance, people who have fallen down the economic ladder or as he terms it, the "new poor".

Racial and religious minorities are also found in mass groups especially those who are partly assimilated into the mainstream as they at times feel left out. Basically, Hoffer argues that misfits or even sinners are most likely to be part of mass movements. They basically follow these movements religiously with the hope of attaining some sense of fulfillment or blaming others for their problems. Take for instance the presidential political campaign by Donald Trump in 2016. True believers insisting that Mexicans drain the economy and frustrate their resources. Mass movements make one lose their sense of identity as an individual and make one focus on his or her identification with the larger communities. Mass movements in a real sense manipulate one's sense of individuality and make one feel awed by just giving the membership to the mass movement.

Mass movements thrive on hatred and their ideal person to direct their hatred to be a foreigner, like for instance, the case of Hitler and the Nazis who turned on the Jews because they were foreigners. This was evident in the Trump's campaign where supporters vigorously advocate for the deportation of "illegal immigrants" who are foreigners to this land. Without a place to redirect their hatred, mass movements are usually ineffective in the long run, they thrive on the hatred as their uniting factor. In the short run however, they can divide a country in racial bounties and inspire prejudice and racism. In cases they did even more damage, leading to killings of everyone perceived as different, culminating in genocides. The most devastating of genocides started with pointing fingers. There is no small case of racism.

Political movements based on race are not new to the USA, however they are new in our era or perceived tolerance and the eradication of racial lines. How did the most popular racial genocides start in other countries? Here is an overview.

Origin and Development of Anti-Semitism in Italy

Italian Jews had achieved acceptance among the Italians and had easily integrated in the society. The result of this was the assimilation of Jews into society as well as the economic and political structure of the nation mainly through business, the civil service and universities. The issue however arose in what the Jewish people stood for which raised a lot of flags. The consequence of Jews was being seen as naturally inclined towards positions that Fascists were opposed and holding beliefs that were defiant, it was a perpetual atmosphere of suspicion of Jewish disloyalty. Fascists endeavored for colonial expansion, a racial form of anti-Semitism began to originate in Italy and slowly crept into the society. Anti-Semitism in Italy was neither an import from Germany nor was it a way of Mussolini showing solidarity with Hitler. It originated from Fascist ideology that saw Jews as possessing traits that were adversative and threatening to Fascism. The racist anti-Semitism that developed in the 1930s originated from a new understanding of race from the Italian colonies, added to the continual pressure of Zionism. This gave rise to the belief that Jews were racially different from Italians and needed separating to protect the future of the nation. Fascism was opposed to liberalism, democracy, Marxism, secularism, and laissez-faire capitalism— and all these aspects, the Jews supported them and thus the Italians began to question their loyalty.

Italian racism has also been useful in scaffolding the national pride, now suffering from an inferiority complex aggravated by the increasingly intimate relationship with the Germans, which in real sense does not benefit Italy in any way.

In the period 1938 to 1943 before Italy lost its sovereignty, the Jews population started facing campaigns against them from Fascist Italy. The passing of anti-Jewish laws that were put forward prior to the Second World War without interference by Germany was a big blow to the Jews community in Italy. Soon thereafter the *Manifesto of Racist Scientists* came in to show the public a theoretical justification as to why an anti-Jewish campaign should be started. This law declared that Jews couldn't have their children sent to private or public schools in Italy. Even textbooks authored by Jewish authors were permanently removed from Italian classrooms. A ban on intermarriages occurring between Aryans and non-Aryans followed. Mussolini wanted to ensure there was purity among the Aryans and no contamination occurred from Jews, who were regarded as inferior people. Such law was stipulated under the "Laws for the Defense of the Race" and had to be fully implemented.

While Mussolini and Italian Fascism might have introduced the anti-Jewish laws in 1938, the ideologies behind it were foreign. How could Italy that had for so long lived harmonious with Jews, suddenly turn their back on them and start discriminating against them? Some people may say that anti-Semitism in Italy was not there and it was brought from outside due to the influence of the Nazi, others think that anti-Semitism thrived in Italy but at a low level until Italians felt that they had enough.

It is of popular view that anti-Semitism had its ideological roots found in Germany and Mussolini was merely being opportunist introducing anti-Jewish laws to further his appeal to Hitler. But in a real sense, is this the case?

Racial Theories in Fascist Italy

Fascism basically operated on the very influential Nazism policies. This was due to the close ties between Italy and Germany. Mussolini founded the first fascist regime, after which others like Nazi Germany followed. Fascism does not take the same identical form in each nation, it differs from one nation to another. Hence, there may be no precise definition of fascism. However, there are common features that try to describe what fascism is and they include absolute power, rule by a dictator, corporatism, extreme nationalism, and superiority of the people of the nation as well as militarism and imperialism.

Before Mussolini was influenced by the ideologies of Hitler, Italy was a peaceful nation and they basically lived well with various people and integrated well.

Italy's leader at that time Benito Mussolini had quite contrasting views when it comes to the significance of race but sometimes he could speak of alarm on extinction of white people, while at other times he could deny the theory of race. The closer ties Mussolini has with Hitler resulted in him sending Jews in Italy to die in Holocaust.

Racism

While race and ethnicity are considered to be separate in contemporary social science, the two terms have a long history of equivalence in popular usage and older social science literature. "Ethnicity" is often used in a sense close to one traditionally attributed to "race": the division of human groups based on qualities assumed to be essential or innate to the group. Racism has always been a big issue to deal with since time immemorial and in most instances, the minority are often picked on and this leads to complete disregard of human life and its dignity and integrity.

Racism and *racial discrimination* are often used to describe discrimination on an ethnic or cultural basis, independent of whether these differences are described as racial.

According to a United Nations Convention, there is no distinction between the terms "racial" and "ethnic" discrimination. The UN Convention further argues that having superiority founded on racial differentiation is pretty scientifically false as well as morally condemnable. It is also socially unjust and perilous. The Convention says that in this world, there isn't justification for racial discrimination whether in theory or in practice.

Today, the use of the term "racism" does not easily fall under a single definition. It is usually found in, but usage is not limited to law, the social and behavioral sciences, humanities, and popular culture. Racism is the belief that characteristics and abilities can be attributed to people simply on the basis of their race and that some racial groups are superior to others.

Racism and discrimination have been used as powerful weapons instilling fear or hatred of others in times of conflict and war, and even during economic downturn. It works to turn on others and is basically fueled by prejudiced actions. From the institutionalized racism especially in colonial times, when racial beliefs even eugenics were not considered something wrong, to recent times where the effects of neo-Nazism are still felt, Europe is a complex area with many cultures in a relatively small area of land that has seen many conflicts throughout history.

Racism, even in its most raw and un-presentable form, is easily utilized as an instrument of containment of social anxieties, and as a means of diverting attention from many failures of national governments in the face of globalization and its economic and political crisis. It is a way or method of running away from responsibilities and placing focus on a different avenue to counter the effect of their failures.

The form of racism maturing today is a dynamic one, creeping and increasingly sophisticated, but no less real and violent. While the Republican Party was famously known for its aggressive fight to end slavery is now on the verge of completely averting all its core values by opposing the proposed immigration reform legislation. The same party whose founding fathers worked hard to establish a name and reputation for standing by and for the minority is slowly changing its focus and embarking on a witch hunt for illegal immigrants. By using the racial card and turning folks against the minority the republicans are using the same tactics used by Hitler and Mussolini, and this is a complete abuse and violation of democracy. The new law has transformed 'unlawful' presence in the territory into a means of reviving the economy with the consequence of increasing the country's GDP and more jobs.

Democracy and Nazism

Democracy entitles people to elect leaders or even tumble them out of power. The population is bestowed power and becomes the sole custodian of authority. Leaders have to seek public approval. Germany practiced a typical democracy, but this ended with the rise of Nazism.

Nazism was among the radical ideologies that appeared in Europe at the start of the World War I. It was established in Germany to advance the interest of the Aryan people.

Another kind of ideology had been started in Italy dubbed the Fascism by Benito Mussolini.

Nazism or National Socialism rejected the fundamental elements of democracy including rationalism, liberalism, rule of law, and human rights often calling for a reconciliation of conservative ideology with the social radical doctrine. Nazism was advocating for oppression and dictatorship. It sought to rule the weak, eradicate any rivalry social, political, and religious institutions.

Hitler's Philosophy

The holocaust brands Hitler as a dictator, but behind him is a philosophy that gives him honorable duty. Hitler through the ideologies of Nazi influenced Fascist Italy to turn against the Jews and send them to the Holocaust to be eliminated. Hitler has a huge following and his ideas seem to have been popular. From Hitler's philosophy, it shows that it is easier for many people to be recruited in supremacist groups. This is especially so if they are recruited at a young age. The kids can follow the ideologies from the young age and grow to be very strong followers. Today, we are witnessing a reincarnation of what happened during the times of Hitler where political candidates like Donald Trump openly disregard the Mexican community in America.

The elements of Nazi ideology were diverse often consisting of German nationalism, racism, anti-Semitism, militarism, socialism, eugenics, genocide imperialistic expansionism, and the "leadership principle".

In his explanation on the philosophy of Nazism, Hitler says that it is paramount for a person to begin to realize that their own ego remains of no importance in the existence of a nation. The position an individual takes is dictated and conditioned merely by the nation's interest.

Hitler's approach to racism, though dreadful, has been emulated by some leaders for example Benito Mussolini of Italy who introduced anti-Semitism to Italy.

The Danger in Political Racial Strategy

I'm listening to the news. The KKK just announced their support of presidential nominee Donald Trump. A Time Magazine article on December 21st 2015 headlined "KKK Leader Finds Donald Trump a Great Recruiting Tool". This after the candidate declares Mexicans are rapists. This ignites a certain percentage of the republican voting population and strengthen Trump's campaign. On the other hand, what does this do to the Republican Party? For years the party has insisted that it needs to attract more Latino voters to ensure its future. This is no great secret; we only need to see the population growth for Latinos in this country to know they'll be the majority soon.

My cousin Eduardo was working a trade show in the Deep South. He's six feet two inches tall with green eyes and jet black hair and fair skin. He approached a distributor to talk about his products and got engaged in conversation.

"What types of stores do you service?" asked Eduardo.
"I call on Convenience stores all over the state," answer the distributor.

After a few questions my cousin introduced himself.
"By the way my name is Eduardo," he said.
"Hello my mane is Billy," said the distributor. A blond, short man wearing a company polo shirt.
"Are you from Spain?" the distributor asked.
"No, I was born in San Diego, my parents are Mexican," he said.

The distributor turned around and gave his back to Eduardo. He didn't want to speak with him anymore, and that was that. Eduardo returned to his booth with the local distributor, an African American. Eduardo explained what happened and his friend could not stop laughing.
"Welcome to the Deep South," he said.

Prejudice Influences Voters for A Long Time

It is clear that during the 2016 presidential campaigning the party of the Latino and the Mexican Americans is the Democratic Party. This if nothing else is by default. We all witnessed the insults to the Latino population, in this case specifically the Mexican Americans and all of their relatives living in Mexico.

The republican candidate Donald Trump started first by instilling fear into the right winged conservative base by blaming all of their problems on a single ethnic group, Mexicans. This is not a new strategy and it's been used by politicians all across time and across the world. Most noticeably in Germany during the Adolph Hitler rule.

The reactions by many on the Republicans was mixed at first, but now a clear divide is emerging with some republicans following Trump and others opposing him. Examination of the Trump phenomenon only creates sadness for this writer. On the one hand, why did the Republican Party elite wait so long to distance themselves from Trump, and on the other, how can so many people overlook his racist and prejudice or dismiss it as "He's not really serious".

Messages of hate and racism are serious not only in principle but in practice. They are also very dangerous when you incite an economically underperforming part of the population to violence. This is a textbook strategy that works in creating political movements followed by votes and then racist segmentation and violence.

Long after Trump is forgotten, or remembered as a circus act the effects of his message of hate will be stamped forever on the Republican Party. Lincoln would be turning in his grave to see the racism planted on his party. The same party that was created to oppose slavery.

What Happened to the Grand Old Party?

The Grand Old Party, GOP or Republican Party was one of the more progressive parties of all time at the moment of its creation in 1854. The party was created to oppose slavery. Stating the argument of "Free Soil, Free Labor, Free Men". An ideology based on ethics and capitalism. The party members saw the free market as a much better solution than one of slavery. This is why they also opposed the expansion of slaves into the new western territories now under American rule after the treaty of Guadalupe.

The Republican Party is among the oldest political parties in the world to be in existence today. It is also the second oldest political party that is existing in America, first being the Democratic Party. The Republican Party was found as a means of protesting the Kansas-Nebraska Act that was said to threaten the extension of slavery and promotion of vibrant modern economy.

With the attaining of power of Abraham Lincoln in 1860, and its victory on abolishing slavery, the party were the top contenders of the national political scene until 1932. The Republicans lost their popularity during the Great Depression. The Democrats then under the leadership of Franklin D. Roosevelt formed a winning coalition, which stayed in power from 1932 till 1964. In the mid-1960s, the Democrats tumbled down due to the dissatisfaction of the white Southern Democrats with the passing of the Civil Rights Act of 1964.

The Republicans came back to the limelight, winning a whopping five of the six presidential elections from 1968 to 1988. Recently their record of presidential election wins is greatly decreasing as from 1992 to 2012, the Republicans have been elected to the White House in only two of the six presidential elections and only in one out of those six elections, in 2004, did they attain popular vote.

The Republicans expanded their membership throughout the South after 1968 mainly due to its immense popularity among Protestants and Roman Catholics. The Democrats began losing popularity in the south and the region began taking on the two party stand which was experienced in most parts of the nation. The Republicans most prominent and influential leader Ronald Reagan conservative policies applied to many as it advocated for reduction of government expenditure and regulation, lowering of taxes, and a powerful policy against the Soviets. He remains popular even into the 21st century as most Republican leaders acknowledge his ideologies. It's ironic that President Regan was pro free trade and opening the border with Mexico as well as the champion of the amnesty program for undocumented immigrants.

The presidential election of Abraham Lincoln in 1860 ended the domination of the coalition of southern Democrats and northern Democrats which had existed since the days of Andrew Jackson. That ushered in a new era of Republican control based in the industrial growth and agriculture dominance.

Lincoln was outstandingly prosperous in helping reconcile the divisions of his party to fight for the Union. However, he experienced a lot of aggression and quite often fought the radicals in the party who demanded harsher measures. Most Democrats initially were War Democrats 1862 after which Lincoln abolished slavery. Many war Democrats thus became "peace Democrats".

The Republican Party has undergone so many transformations since its date of formation and through-out its evolution one of the most iconic and influential leaders was Ronald Reagan. What attracted many to his ideas was his social conservatism especially on contentious matters such as abortion. He reinvented American politics. He worked to reinstate America's economy and did so by cutting the taxes down by 25% and abolishing of upper taxes. His leadership tactics still appeal to many.

In a drastic turn of events, the Republican party in just half a century has shifted its base from regions of the industrial Northeast and urban centers and established roots in the South and West. This results in Republicans electing more populist, anti-tax and anti-government conservatives who are not supportive and are very suspicious of appeals from big business and thus completely disorients their focus.

Marketing To Latinos

Latinos have very wide networks of friends and family. Making them superconductors of information and political recommendations, or on the other hand, political opposition.

Many political analysts will argue that having their support will be a huge benefit to the campaigns. Thus the republican's decision to go against the new immigration reform automatically withdrew all Latinos support from the political party. About 24 million Latinos are eligible to vote thus they are a crucial group. It should be noted that the Latinos helped reelect Obama.

The focus mainly should be on how to appeal to this particular group of people. A few tricks include; live interactions with them where a candidate is subjected to answer question about their policies and how it will benefit them. Another important aspect is to arrange one's ideologies to suit their needs. For instance, Latinos are more concerned with immigration and other important matters like economy and education according to Pew research center thus if you want to have your way with the Latino votes, be sure to tackle the immigration grievances as fear of deportation is faced by most of them.

The approach to marketing in politics and in selling has varied over the years. One true thing about marketing is the golden rule: Know Your Market. We've spent a long time and effort researching and explaining the culture and mentality of the North American Latino for a reason: to give you a glimpse into your target market. This is so you can better understand, and in turn communicate your message and establish a connection, maybe even an emotional connection with your target market.

Here are some recommendations:

Extended Networks: Remember Latinos don't have a small network of friends and family. They have a large one, potentially hundreds of members in their immediate circle when you consider extended family and friends. If your campaign works with misinformation you can be a victim of fact-checking and then banned from the Latino network. If you use typical target market information segmentation it can come back to banned your candidate form the Latino support. For example, if your candidate asks for the Latino vote in one meeting, and then threatens to deport immigrants and raise the American Wall, whether you think it's controversial or not, it is to Latinos.

Prejudice and Short Term vs. Long Term Strategy

The fact that candidates are mostly responsible for their election and campaign as well as their strategy makes the strategy by default a short term one. If a party has a consensus that it will target Latinos in the long term it becomes meaningless if the current candidate doesn't appeal to the segment, or doesn't care for it. Or worse, the candidate has anti-Latino sentiment in a direct or indirect way.

In other countries such as Mexico the party has much more control over the message and strategy of the campaign and the candidates. The national party sets the values and strategy, then it goes down to the states, and then the city offices. Members of the party have meetings to go over strategies and values since they are young members or activists. Volunteers and party members are not to support one member, but the philosophy of the party.

In contrast, a US political candidate has almost complete autonomy over his campaign and message. If the message goes against that of the party, the nominee could still be successful if he or she can gather enough public support.

A long term strategy to campaigning includes a nurturing period to establish rapport. This means you can't contact a potential Latino voter by phone tomorrow and ask them to vote for your candidate. Especially with Latinos establishing a relationship is very important. The culture is one of connections and relationships.

Once you win the confidence of a Latino voter you'll be rewarded with a connector, a supporter that will convince ten, twenty, maybe thirty people of your message. Not just in one election but in every election. Latinos are loyal by culture. That's why they root for their national soccer team besides the US team. This is true not just for sports or politics but also for business. Service providers and small businesses are aware that if you can acquire a Latino customer for the business you'll acquire all their friends and their family.

Final Note. When I Was Deported

After eight years of thinking about this book I finally decided to write it. The main motivation was all the misinformation and propaganda about immigration, Latinos and their role in the US economy, society and politics.

My love of culture propelled me to write about history, ethnicity and society. What I saw on the news gave me the courage to speak up with facts, not soundbites. My own experience gave me the unique view and position to write The Latino Vote.

Laws are made by man, no matter how much politicians pray or want to link divine intervention in their campaign. These laws are written by those in power at that particular time. Many times placing their future in politics before the wellbeing of all others. So history is made, with those laws in the middle. These laws and this history shape the US and how Latinos are seen in it.

Laws are imperfect. They can catalog good people as illegals, they can separate children form their mothers, and in my case, they can deport US Citizens.

The Deportation of This Author

When I was seventeen years old my uncle Pepe came into my room in my home in Tijuana, Mexico.

"Jorge, do you know you're American Citizen?" He asked.

I looked at him with some confusion. My mind racing to understand how I could be an American Citizen if I was born in Mexico.

"Because my father is an American?" I gave as my best guest.

"That's right" he said. "You can go to the university in the US and work in the US if you want to.

"Why would I want to do that" I thought. After all, it was the summer of 1989 and next year I would be a senior in high school, captain of the basketball team, and would graduate from a religious school after twelve years of attendance. There was to be a dedicated ceremony with special honors. I was very excited.

My uncle lived in the USA, he had a green card and knew the benefits of studying and working in the county. "You can come back if you don't like it, but if you don't go, you could be missing an opportunity and will never know it" he told me.

We talked for another hour about the US, universities in the country and the level of education. "I'll think about it" I told him at the end.

Before this moment I never considered going to the US. I was happy in Mexico, happy with my friends, with my family and with my prospects for work. The fact that I was a US citizen because my father is an American never crossed my mind.

I thought about this for the rest of the day and slept on it. The next day I decided to go to the USA and leave my school, my basketball team, my church and my friends. I never even had a chance to say good bye to them because I left before the school year.

At first I crossed the border daily. Trekking from my house in Tijuana all the way to school in the US using public transportation in both countries. I walked a mile, took a bus to downtown Tijuana, waited in line, crossed the border, took the trolley and then another bus to school. It was a two hour affair each way.

At the same time I contacted the US immigration service to find out how to get my documents as a US citizen. They started the process and informed me that I was a citizen by "Derived Citizenship" from my father. This is the same type of citizenship Senator and Presidential Candidate Ted Cruz has.

One of those days as I crossed the border to go to school I was stopped and sent to secondary inspection.

"Where are you going?" the office asked me.

"I'm going to school" I said, backpack full of books in my hand.

"You can't go to school, that's illegal" he said.

After all, my only means of identification was my Mexican passport with a US tourist visa. You can't go to school with a tourist visa. I was nervous and my hands were shaking while I explained to the uniformed officer I was a US citizen and as such I could go to school in the USA.

"You're breaking the law. You are now considered an illegal in this country" he responded firmly.

Again, I tried to explain I was a US citizen and if he just checked… "I don't care what you are. And if you keep talking I'll put you in jail" he said.

My breath was lost. I was seventeen and I knew in Mexico he could do that. I knew my rights on that side of the border. At seventeen, a minor, they had to call my parents if I broke the law. However I didn't know my rights in the US, I didn't know the law. I couldn't call a lawyer and dint' know anyone in the US besides my Uncle. By now I was holding my tears the best I could. I watched while he stamped CANCELED on my Visa.

"Go back to Mexico" he said. "You're lucky I'm letting you go".

I cried all the way back home. "They don't want me in that country" I thought. I have a Mexican sounding name and an accent so they don't want me". I wondered what I was to do now. I already left my old life, my friends, school, everything.

The next day I left my passport at home along with all my identifications and headed for the border. Waited in line to cross and when I came to the immigration inspector told him "US Citizen".

Endnotes

1   LA Times, "It's official: Latinos now outnumber whites in California" available at http://www.latimes.com/local/california/la-me-census-latinos-20150708-story.html

2   LA Times, "It's official: Latinos now outnumber whites in California" available at http://www.latimes.com/local/california/la-me-census-latinos-20150708-story.html

3   LA Times, "It's official: Latinos now outnumber whites in California" available at http://www.latimes.com/local/california/la-me-census-latinos-20150708-story.html

4   LA Times, "It's official: Latinos now outnumber whites in California" available at http://www.latimes.com/local/california/la-me-census-latinos-20150708-story.html

5   LA Times, "It's official: Latinos now outnumber whites in California" available at http://www.latimes.com/local/california/la-me-census-latinos-20150708-story.html

6   LA Times, "It's official: Latinos now outnumber whites in California" available at http://www.latimes.com/local/california/la-me-census-latinos-20150708-story.html

7   LA Times, "It's official: Latinos now outnumber whites in California" available at http://www.latimes.com/local/california/la-me-census-latinos-20150708-story.html

8   LA Times, "It's official: Latinos now outnumber whites in California" available at http://www.latimes.com/local/california/la-me-census-latinos-20150708-story.html

9   USA Today, "Hispanic vote will reach record high in 2016" available at http://www.usatoday.com/story/news/politics/elections/2016/2016/01/19/hispanic-vote-pew-research-center-report-2016-election/79003656/

10 USA Today, "Hispanic vote will reach record high in 2016" available at http://www.usatoday.com/story/news/politics/elections/2016/2016/01/19/hispanic-vote-pew-research-center-report-2016-election/79003656/

11 Pewhispanic.org, "Millennials Make Up Almost Half of Latino Eligible Voters in 2016" available at http://www.pewhispanic.org/2016/01/19/millennials-make-up-almost-half-of-latino-eligible-voters-in-2016/

12 USA Today, "Hispanic vote will reach record high in 2016" available at http://www.usatoday.com/story/news/politics/elections/2016/2016/01/19/hispanic-vote-pew-research-center-report-2016-election/79003656/

13 USA Today, "Hispanic vote will reach record high in 2016" available at http://www.usatoday.com/story/news/politics/elections/2016/2016/01/19/hispanic-vote-pew-research-center-report-2016-election/79003656/

14 USA Today, "Hispanic vote will reach record high in 2016" available at http://www.usatoday.com/story/news/politics/elections/2

016/2016/01/19/hispanic-vote-pew-research-center-report-2016-election/79003656/

15 USA Today, "Hispanic vote will reach record high in 2016" available at http://www.usatoday.com/story/news/politics/elections/2016/2016/01/19/hispanic-vote-pew-research-center-report-2016-election/79003656/

16 USA Today, "Hispanic vote will reach record high in 2016" available at http://www.usatoday.com/story/news/politics/elections/2016/2016/01/19/hispanic-vote-pew-research-center-report-2016-election/79003656/

17 USA Today, "Hispanic vote will reach record high in 2016" available at http://www.usatoday.com/story/news/politics/elections/2016/2016/01/19/hispanic-vote-pew-research-center-report-2016-election/79003656/

18 USA Today, "Hispanic vote will reach record high in 2016" available at http://www.usatoday.com/story/news/politics/elections/2016/2016/01/19/hispanic-vote-pew-research-center-report-2016-election/79003656/

19 PewResearch.org, "Democratic edge in Hispanic voter registration grows in Florida" available at http://www.pewresearch.org/fact-tank/2016/03/09/democratic-edge-in-hispanic-voter-registration-grows-in-florida/

20 PewResearch.org, "Democratic edge in Hispanic voter registration grows in Florida" available at http://www.pewresearch.org/fact-tank/2016/03/09/democratic-edge-in-hispanic-voter-registration-grows-in-florida/

21 PewResearch.org, "Democratic edge in Hispanic voter registration grows in Florida" available at http://www.pewresearch.org/fact-tank/2016/03/09/democratic-edge-in-hispanic-voter-registration-grows-in-florida/

22 PewResearch.org, "Democratic edge in Hispanic voter registration grows in Florida" available at http://www.pewresearch.org/fact-tank/2016/03/09/democratic-edge-in-hispanic-voter-registration-grows-in-florida/

23 Chu A. and Posner C. "How the Rising Share of Latino Voters Will Impact the 2016 Elections," 2015 available at https://cdn.americanprogress.org/wp-content/uploads/2015/12/08050053/LatinoPoliticalPower1.pdf

24 Americanprogress.org, "Top 6 Facts on the Latino Vote" available at https://www.americanprogress.org/issues/immigration/news/2015/09/17/121325/top-6-facts-on-the-latino-vote/

25 Americanprogress.org, "Top 6 Facts on the Latino Vote" available at https://www.americanprogress.org/issues/immigration/news/2015/09/17/121325/top-6-facts-on-the-latino-vote/

26 Americanprogress.org, "Top 6 Facts on the Latino Vote" available at https://www.americanprogress.org/issues/immigration/news/2015/09/17/121325/top-6-facts-on-the-latino-vote/

27 Americanprogress.org, "Top 6 Facts on the Latino Vote" available at https://www.americanprogress.org/issues/immigration/news/2015/09/17/121325/top-6-facts-on-the-latino-vote/

28 Americanprogress.org, "Top 6 Facts on the Latino Vote" available at https://www.americanprogress.org/issues/immigration/news/2015/09/17/121325/top-6-facts-on-the-latino-vote/

29 Americanprogress.org, "Top 6 Facts on the Latino Vote" available at https://www.americanprogress.org/issues/immigration/news/2015/09/17/121325/top-6-facts-on-the-latino-vote/

30 Americanprogress.org, "Top 6 Facts on the Latino Vote" available at https://www.americanprogress.org/issues/immigration/news/2015/09/17/121325/top-6-facts-on-the-latino-vote/

31 Chu A. and Posner C. "How the Rising Share of Latino Voters Will Impact the 2016 Elections," 2015 available at https://cdn.americanprogress.org/wp-content/uploads/2015/12/08050053/LatinoPoliticalPower1.pdf

32 Chu A. and Posner C. "How the Rising Share of Latino Voters Will Impact the 2016 Elections," 2015

33 Chu A. and Posner C. "How the Rising Share of Latino Voters Will Impact the 2016 Elections," 2015

34 Chu A. and Posner C. "How the Rising Share of Latino Voters Will Impact the 2016 Elections," 2015

35 Chu A. and Posner C. "How the Rising Share of Latino Voters Will Impact the 2016 Elections," 2015

36 Chu A. and Posner C. "How the Rising Share of Latino Voters Will Impact the 2016 Elections," 2015

37 Chu A. and Posner C. "How the Rising Share of Latino Voters Will Impact the 2016 Elections," 2015

38 Chu A. and Posner C. "How the Rising Share of Latino Voters Will Impact the 2016 Elections," 2015

39 Chu A. and Posner C. "How the Rising Share of Latino Voters Will Impact the 2016 Elections," 2015

40 Chu A. and Posner C. "How the Rising Share of Latino Voters Will Impact the 2016 Elections," 2015

41 Chu A. and Posner C. "How the Rising Share of Latino Voters Will Impact the 2016 Elections," 2015

42 Chu A. and Posner C. "How the Rising Share of Latino Voters Will Impact the 2016 Elections," 2015

43 *Wall Street Journal* " How Latinos Power the American Economy" available at http://www.wsj.com/articles/how-latinos-power-the-american-economy-1457907023

44 *Wall Street Journal* " How Latinos Power the American Economy" available at http://www.wsj.com/articles/how-latinos-power-the-american-economy-1457907023

45 *Wall Street Journal* " How Latinos Power the American Economy" available at http://www.wsj.com/articles/how-latinos-power-the-american-economy-1457907023

46 *Wall Street Journal* " How Latinos Power the American Economy" available at http://www.wsj.com/articles/how-latinos-power-the-american-economy-1457907023

47 PewHispanic.org, "State and County Databases" available at http://www.pewhispanic.org/states/

48 PewHispanic.org, "Mapping the Latino Electorate by Congressional District" available at http://www.pewhispanic.org/interactives/mapping-the-latino-electorate-by-congressional-district/

49 PewHispanic.org, "Mapping the Latino Electorate by State"

http://www.pewhispanic.org/interactives/mapping-the-latino-electorate-by-state/

50 House.gov, "Directory of Representatives" available at http://www.house.gov/representatives/

51 John A. Garcia, Gabriel R. Sanchez, J. Salvador Peralta "Latino Politics: A Growing and Evolving Political Community"

52 Lana Baker-Cowling, "The Spanish Conquest of South America... Genocide?" available at https://prezi.com/em0nh-ehsvr4/the-spanish-conquest-of-south-america-genocide/

53 Colin A. Palmer, "A Legacy Of Slavery" available at http://www.smithsonianeducation.org/migrations/legacy/almleg.html

54 Encyclopedia, "Latinos: Encyclopedia of World Cultures" available at http://www.encyclopedia.com/topic/Latinos.aspx#1

55 *The Christian Post,* "If Latinos Are Conservative, Why Do They Vote Democrat? (Video Interview)" available at http://www.christianpost.com/news/if-latinos-are-conservative-why-do-they-vote-democrat-video-interview-122078/#DyId016YCIkwqtVx.99

56 Pewforum.org, "The Shifting Religious Identity of Latinos in the United States" available at http://www.pewforum.org/2014/05/07/the-shifting-religious-identity-of-latinos-in-the-united-states/

57 *The Guardian,* "Most Hispanics vote Democrat, so why are so many Hispanic politicians Republican?" available at http://www.theguardian.com/commentisfree/2015/nov/18/most-hispanics-vote-democrat-but-most-hispanic-politicians-are-republican-marco-rubio-ted-cruz

58 Pew Hispanic.org, "When Labels Don't Fit: Hispanics and Their Views of Identity V. Politics, Values and Religion" available at http://www.pewhispanic.org/2012/04/04/v-politics-values-and-religion/

59 Pew Hispanic.org, "When Labels Don't Fit: Hispanics and Their Views of Identity V. Politics, Values and Religion" available at http://www.pewhispanic.org/2012/04/04/v-politics-values-and-religion/

60 Pew Hispanic.org, "When Labels Don't Fit: Hispanics and Their Views of Identity V. Politics, Values and Religion" available at http://www.pewhispanic.org/2012/04/04/v-politics-values-and-religion/

61 Pew Hispanic.org, "When Labels Don't Fit: Hispanics and Their Views of Identity V. Politics, Values and Religion" available at http://www.pewhispanic.org/2012/04/04/v-politics-values-and-religion/

62 Pew Hispanic.org, "When Labels Don't Fit: Hispanics and Their Views of Identity V. Politics, Values and Religion" available at http://www.pewhispanic.org/2012/04/04/v-politics-values-and-religion/

63 Pew Hispanic.org, "When Labels Don't Fit: Hispanics and Their Views of Identity V. Politics, Values and Religion" available at http://www.pewhispanic.org/2012/04/04/v-politics-values-and-religion/

64 Pbs.org, "Latino-americans:Timeline of Important Dates" available at http://www.pbs.org/latino-americans/en/timeline/

65 Pbs.org, "Latino-americans:Timeline of Important Dates" available at http://www.pbs.org/latino-americans/en/timeline/

66 Pbs.org, "Latino-americans:Timeline of Important Dates" available at http://www.pbs.org/latino-americans/en/timeline/

67 Pbs.org, "Latino-americans:Timeline of Important Dates" available at http://www.pbs.org/latino-americans/en/timeline/

68 Pbs.org, "Latino-americans:Timeline of Important Dates" available at http://www.pbs.org/latino-americans/en/timeline/

69 Pbs.org, "Latino-americans:Timeline of Important Dates" available at http://www.pbs.org/latino-americans/en/timeline/

70 Pbs.org, "Latino-americans:Timeline of Important Dates" available at http://www.pbs.org/latino-americans/en/timeline/

71 Loc.gov, "Becoming Part of the United States" available at http://www.loc.gov/teachers/classroommaterials/presentationsandactivities/presentations/immigration/mexican2.html

72 Loc.gov, "Becoming Part of the United States" available at http://www.loc.gov/teachers/classroommaterials/presentationsandactivities/presentations/immigration/mexican2.html

73 Nps.gov, "An Historic Overview of Latino Immigration
and the Demographic Transformation of the United
States" available at
https://www.nps.gov/heritageinitiatives/latino/latinothem
estudy/immigration.htm

74 Nps.gov, "An Historic Overview of Latino Immigration
and the Demographic Transformation of the United
States" available at
https://www.nps.gov/heritageinitiatives/latino/latinothem
estudy/immigration.htm

75 Nps.gov, "An Historic Overview of Latino Immigration
and the Demographic Transformation of the United
States" available at
https://www.nps.gov/heritageinitiatives/latino/latinothem
estudy/immigration.htm

76 Nps.gov, "An Historic Overview of Latino Immigration
and the Demographic Transformation of the United
States" available at
https://www.nps.gov/heritageinitiatives/latino/latinothem
estudy/immigration.htm

77 Nps.gov, "An Historic Overview of Latino Immigration
and the Demographic Transformation of the United
States" available at
https://www.nps.gov/heritageinitiatives/latino/latinothem
estudy/immigration.htm

78 Nps.gov, "An Historic Overview of Latino Immigration
and the Demographic Transformation of the United
States" available at
https://www.nps.gov/heritageinitiatives/latino/latinothem
estudy/immigration.htm

79 Nps.gov, "An Historic Overview of Latino Immigration
and the Demographic Transformation of the United

States" available at
https://www.nps.gov/heritageinitiatives/latino/latinothem
estudy/immigration.htm

80 *Wall Street Journal*, "Should Washington End
Agriculture Subsidies?"
http://www.wsj.com/articles/should-washington-end-
agriculture-subsidies-1436757020

81 Udel.edu, "A brief history of the Mason-Dixon Line"
available at
http://www.udel.edu/johnmack/mason_dixon/

82 Theamericanwall.com, "The American Wall : From The
Pacific Ocean to The Gulf of Mexico" available at
http://theamericanwall.com/index.php/about-us/

83 Cbsnews.com, "A New Direction On Drugs" available
at http://www.cbsnews.com/news/60-minutes-a-new-
direction-on-drugs/

84 Drugpolicy.org, "The Federal Drug Control Budget:
New Rhetoric, Same Failed Drug War" available at
http://www.drugpolicy.org/sites/default/files/DPA_Fact_
sheet_Drug_War_Budget_Feb2015.pdf

85 Usimmigration.com , "The Costs and Benefits of Border
Security" available at
https://www.usimmigration.com/cost-benefits-border-
security.html

86 Usatoday.com, "Obama administration spent $18B on
immigration enforcement" available at
http://www.usatoday.com/story/news/nation/2013/01/07/
obama-immigration-enforcement/1815667/

87 Dhs.gov, "Budget in Brief Fiscal Year 2014: Homeland
Security"
https://www.dhs.gov/sites/default/files/publications/MG

MT/FY%202014%20BIB%20-%20FINAL%20-508%20Formatted%20(4).pdf

88 Isreview.org, "The political economy of Mexico's drug war" available at http://isreview.org/issue/90/political-economy-mexicos-drug-war

89 Ncjrs.gov, "A Comprehensive Approach: Reducing the Supply of Illegal Drugs" available at https://www.ncjrs.gov/ondcppubs/publications/policy/99ndcs/iv-g.html

90 Drugabuse.gov, "DrugFacts: Nationwide Trends" available at https://www.drugabuse.gov/publications/drugfacts/nationwide-trends

91 Justice.gov, "The Economic Impact of Illicit Drug Use on American Society" available at https://www.justice.gov/archive/ndic/pubs44/44731/44731p.pdf

Index

illegal immigration, 15, 144,
161, 162, 175, 181, 182, 195,
239, 240
immigrant generation., 150
immigrant workers, 171, 281
immigrants are bad people,
139
immigration bill, 173, 283
Immigration policies, 155
immigration status, 64, 161,
281
impermanent Mexican
workers, 158
import 200,000 to 500,000, 88
indigenous cultures, 109
indigenous Indians fled, 89
indigenous people died, 91
Indigenous Population, 94
influence Latinos, 86
influence the Latinos, 31, 156
inventors of slavery, 88

J

Jan Brewer, 128, 162
jeopardizing the security, 208
Job opportunities, 155
John Perez, 74
jungle and canyons, 89
Justice of the Supreme Court,
76

K

keep drugs out, 215, 216
Keep Out, 201
higher Hispanic eligible
populations, 64
key battleground states, 36
kidnappings 207
killing Latinos, 202
kingmaker 67
KKK, 202, 307

L

labor agreement, 160, 170, 178
labor force, 162, 178, 179,
258, 287, 289, 292, 295
laborers in textile factories, 91
landmark legislation, 127
large disparity, 293
large population, 70
larger young population, 58
largest consumption of drugs,
227
largest ethnic group, 21
largest Hispanic eligible voter,
61
largest minority group, 66
largest population of Latinos,
23
largest share of eligible
minority, 47
Latin American governments,
179
Latin American heritage, 132
Latin American immigrants,
142, 163, 164
Latin American migration, 169
Latinisation 65, 75
Latino American immigrants,
101
Latino Catholics, 149, 150,
154
Latino culture, 106, 138
Latino Electorate by State, 64
Latino electorate, 34
Latino eligible voters, 54
Latino ethnic identity, 102
Latino immigrants, 55
Latino Pentecostals, 149
Latino values, 107
Latino voters influence the
California law makers, 10
Latino voters, 34, 35

Want to Continue The Conversation?

Contact Jorge to continue the conversation on The Latino Vote, Immigration, or Marketing to Latinos.

Jorge is available for interviews, keynotes and other speaking engagements.

Contact him at:
www.JorgeOlson.com